TRUST THYSELF

TRUST THYSELF

Thomas Jefferson wrote the Declaration of Independence. Ralph Waldo Emerson wrote America's intellectual Declaration of Independence from the Old World and delivered it as an unforgettable address at Harvard in 1837. Other men cleared America's forests, fought and won her wars, built her railroads, gave body to the new country. Emerson gave that body soul and spirit.

Tall, thin, with the face of an angel, Emerson wrote like an angel, and he wrote about one thing: the divine in man, man's soul, man's spirit. He was a poet and a priest of beauty who walked with his head in the clouds and his eyes on the stars, but with his feet firmly on the ground.

In Concord, Massachusetts, where he lived almost all his life, he was the generous friend and teacher of Amos Bronson Alcott and Henry David Thoreau, the revered master of Louisa M. Alcott, and sometimes the companion of the lonely Nathaniel Hawthorne. In Boston and Cambridge he was the close friend of Henry Wadsworth Longfellow, James Russell Lowell, and Oliver Wendell Holmes. In England he knew William Wordsworth, Samuel Taylor Coleridge, and Thomas De Quincey, and he was the lifelong intimate of the fiery Thomas Carlyle.

There was a radiance about Ralph Waldo Emerson, as there is about his words, yet he was a plain and practical nineteenth-century New Englander and at the same time a traveled man of the larger world.

The whole Emerson, the poet who wrote that beauty is its own excuse for being and the Massachusetts Yankee who insisted on pie for breakfast, emerges from the clear pages of this new biography.

Also by James Playsted Wood
A Hound, a Bay Horse, and a Turtle-Dove

TRUST THYSELF

A Life of Ralph Waldo Emerson
for the Young Reader

JAMES PLAYSTED WOOD

Illustrations by
Douglas Gorsline

PANTHEON BOOKS

"for E.C.W."

FIRST PRINTING

All the mistakes I make arise from forsaking my own station and trying to see the object from another person's point of view.

Journal, April 12, 1834

I will trust my instincts.

Journal, May 21, 1834

In all my lectures I have taught one doctrine, namely, the infinitude of the private man.

Journal, April 7, 1840

Build therefore your own world.

Nature, 1836

In self-trust all the virtues are comprehended.

"The American Scholar," 1837

Trust thyself: every heart vibrates to that iron string.

"Self-Reliance," 1841

Insist on yourself; never imitate.

"Self-Reliance"

Grateful acknowledgment is made to the Houghton Mifflin Company for permission to quote from the writings of Ralph Waldo Emerson.

TRUST THYSELF

1

The United States was a very young country when Ralph Waldo Emerson was born. The Revolutionary War had ended only twenty years before. The Constitution, adopted in 1787, had been in effect only sixteen years. The United States was a raw, new country, poor and struggling to be rich, weak and struggling to be strong. With fewer than six million people, and most of these in the cities, towns, and villages along the Atlantic coast, it was small, yet determined to be as large as the new continent it occupied and larger than its dreams and ambitions. Reckless and boastful, the lusty young country had nerves and muscles that it was avid to try and more than enough energy to make good its boasts of physical strength and material growth.

That along with its charging advance toward material riches and success the young country developed a literary culture, an appreciation of the scholar as well as of the farmer, merchant, and mechanic; that it retained its ideals and remembered its spiritual values, is due as much to Ralph Waldo Emerson as to any other one man. Religious forces— the dominant Puritanism in New England, Quakerism in Pennsylvania, Roman Catholicism in Maryland, and Anglicanism in Virginia—had been strong in the United States since the founding of the original European settlements out of which it emerged. Yet Emerson did more perhaps than such diverse religious leaders as the Mathers, Jonathan Edwards, George Whitefield, John Woolman, and their successors to give the young country soul and mind as well as body. That despite the international political struggles, the mass movements and the mass thinking which compel and largely control life in the United States now, the individual still exists and the right of the individual to think and feel for himself is still valued is the achievement of men like Ralph Waldo Emerson.

Through his life, through his speech, through his writings in prose and verse, Emerson warmed men's spirits, reached their hearts, and lighted their minds. The nobility of his thought and his inspiriting expression of fundamental truths as he saw them have heartened and uplifted men and women for more than a century. He showed people a new way of looking at themselves and at life about them. He inspired countless writers and teachers. Emerson left a different world than he found, and part of that difference he brought about. That is no mean accomplishment.

Ralph Waldo Emerson breathed new life into his own generation. He brought new hope, new understanding, new and exciting awareness of what life could mean, to men and women, especially young men and women, in his native New England, throughout the East, and in what was in his time the West. He stimulated writers and scholars to new and great effort, and ordinary men and women to realize a beauty in the world and in their own minds and souls that they had not seen or imagined before he showed it to them. Wherever he went throughout his life, he affected people in a way that they could not always understand. They felt something magical in his presence and heard the music of the spheres in his grave voice. Wherever they were read, his essays and his poetry stimulated and excited. They still do. On its highest moral and spiritual levels, American life was, in essence, changed because Emerson lived.

The vital, unformed United States may have been new when Ralph Waldo Emerson was born in Boston in 1803, but New England was already an old, long-settled part of the American continent. The Commonwealth of Massachusetts was only seventeen years old, but the Massachusetts Bay Colony had a long history under British rule. The Pilgrims had landed at Plymouth in 1620. The Puritans had first come in 1628, and founded Boston in 1630. Massachusetts, in fact, still has almost as long a history as an English colony as it has as a state of the United States, and Emerson's Puritan ancestors had been important in Massachusetts almost from the very first.

Among the Puritans who came to the colony in 1635 were Thomas Emerson of York or Durham in England and the Reverend Peter Bulkeley. Thomas Emerson, who settled in Ipswich, is said to have been a baker, but Peter Bulkeley, like his father before him, was a priest of the Church of England, a rector in Bedfordshire. Because of his puritanical beliefs, he refused to wear a surplice in the pulpit or to make the sign of the cross in baptism. As a result, he was suspended and ordered to appear before the High Commission Court if he did not mend his ways. Instead, Peter Bulkeley sold his substantial estates and set sail for New England. He spent about a year in Cambridge, just across the Charles River from Boston. He then bought land from the Indians on the Musketaquid River, about twenty miles northwest of Boston, founded the village of Concord, and became its first minister.

The Puritans had emigrated from England to New England for religious reasons. They wished to worship in their own severe way, to purify the English church of forms and rituals in which they did not believe. Followers of John Calvin, the Protestant reformer, they were literal in their interpretation of the Bible, stern and strict in the conduct they demanded of themselves and all about them.

They believed, among other things, that man is by nature bad. They believed that some people would be saved and achieve grace and everlasting life in heaven, but that others, regardless of their conduct on earth, would not. Only those whom God chose would achieve this salvation. Others could have no hope of obtaining it. They believed that the Church should rule in all matters, temporal as well as spiritual. Thus, early New England was a theocracy, a state in which the Church ruled. Its ministers were powerful. They governed as well as led their people.

Emerson's ancestor Peter Bulkeley was one of these Puritan "divines." He has been described as the patron saint of Concord, a ministerial monarch of the village. When he died in 1659, he was succeeded by his son, the Reverend Edward Bulkeley.

Meanwhile, Thomas Emerson's son had become the minister of Mendon, Massachusetts. When Mendon was attacked by Indians and destroyed, he fled to Concord and there married Elizabeth Bulkeley, the daughter of Edward Bulkeley. Five of the first twelve ministers of Concord were either Bulkeleys or Emersons. More Emersons were ministers in other Massachusetts towns and villages about Boston. Ralph Waldo Emerson's grandfather, the Reverend William Emerson, was the Concord minister when the Revolutionary War broke out. An impassioned patriot, he immediately joined the Continental Army as a chaplain in 1776. He died of fever while on service in Rutland, Vermont, the next year.

His son, another William Emerson, was the father of Ralph Waldo Emerson. Born in Concord in 1769, he graduated from Harvard and became the minister of Harvard, Massachusetts.

As the seventeenth century passed and the eighteenth century wore on into the nineteenth, Puritanism became

6

less severe. Stringent beliefs were softened. The conduct of life was less rigid. Temporal power passed from ministers into the hands of laymen. The idealism and the poetry that had always existed at the heart of Puritanism became more manifest than its harshness. As generation succeeded generation, the Harvard-educated, ministerial Emersons seem to have been each time on the more liberal side. They were scholars and writers as well as preachers, and modern in their views.

William Emerson was a minister of this kind. He was a Unitarian minister, and Unitarianism was the most advanced and liberal-minded of the various Protestant denominations into which the original Puritan church had divided and developed. Social, musical, and literary in his tastes, William Emerson married Ruth Haskins, daughter of a Boston merchant, in 1796. His ministerial salary at Harvard was small, but he taught school on the side, as so many of the Emersons did, and worked on his small farm. "We are poor and cold, and have little meal, and little wood, and little meat, but, thank God, courage enough," he wrote in one letter. The Reverend William Emerson was always optimistic.

In 1799 his fortunes suddenly changed for the better. His father had been an army chaplain. The son was chaplain of the Ancient and Honorable Artillery Company of Boston. As such, he was invited to preach at the important First Church in the city when the Company held services on choosing its officers. William Emerson made so favorable an impression that within a week he was offered the pastorate of Boston's leading church. So anxious was its congregation to obtain his services that it paid a thousand dollars to the Unitarian church in Harvard to help it meet the expense of hiring a new minister.

Tall, fair, handsome, a man of striking appearance with the melodious speaking voice which his son inherited, William Emerson had already thought of leaving Harvard.

7

He had planned to found a new church in the new city of Washington, D.C., a church which would have no written creed, no confession of faith, and ask no statement of belief before admitting anyone to communion. This was very advanced religious thought at that time.

Emerson's father was popular in Boston. He liked to mingle with people. He attended all the social events he could manage. He was happy at the First Church and happy, by his own declaration, in all he did. He lived, he wrote, in "an ample and beautiful world in which there has been afforded me a pleasant lot and much happiness, worthy friends, and delightful contemplations."

He was a founder of the Philosophical Society. He founded the Christian Ministers Society for the publication of religious pamphlets. He was an active member of the Massachusetts Historical Society. He helped found the Anthology Club, whose collection of books grew into the well-known Boston Athenaeum. He was chaplain of the Massachusetts State Senate. He wrote *An Historical Sketch of the First Church in Boston,* edited a hymnal, and published various sermons and addresses. He was the editor of *The Monthly Anthology.* This literary magazine, to which judges, lawyers, ministers, and even a future President of the United States contributed, was considered Boston's best intellectual and cultural publication.

May 25, 1803, this busy minister, editor, and gentleman about Boston noted in his diary—evidently in what he considered the order of their importance—the events of his day: "Mr. Puffer preached his Election Sermon to great acceptance. This day also, whilst I was at dinner at Governor Strong's, my son Ralph Waldo was born. Mrs. E. well. Club at Mr. Adams'."

An admired and gracious figure about Boston, the Reverend William Emerson was not too provident a husband. It did not worry him unduly. Even when he grew ill and suspected that the illness might be serious, he wrote a

8

friend that he felt no great concern for his young family. God only knew, he said, how they would subsist and how the children would be educated, but, "our family, you know, have so long been in the habit of trusting Providence that none of them ever seriously thought of providing a terrestrial maintenance for themselves and households." He died in May 1811, when he was forty-two and his fourth child and third son, Ralph Waldo, was eight.

Emerson remembered little of his father. He did remember that the Ancient and Honorable Artillery Company followed their chaplain to the graveside, and, boylike, he was pleased with the military display. He remembered something else not quite as pleasant. Charming as he had been to the world, William Emerson had been rather a severe father. Several times he had thrown the small boy into what Emerson years later described as "mortal terror" by forcing him into the salt water off some wharf or bathing house. "I still remember," Emerson wrote, "the fright with which, after some of these salt water experiences, I heard his voice one day (as Adam that of the Lord God in the garden) summoning me to a new bath, and I vainly endeavoring to hide myself."

The Emersons had had eight children. They were Phebe Ripley, John Clarke, William, Ralph Waldo, Edward Bliss, Robert Bulkeley, Charles Chauncey, and Mary Caroline. Their first child, born in Harvard, died the year after the Emersons went to Boston; the last child, born about the time of the father's death, died early. Five boys survived their father. They were William, Edward, Robert, Charles, and Ralph Waldo. Four of them, William, Ralph Waldo, Edward, and Charles, were considered bright and promising. The fifth, Robert Bulkeley, was mentally retarded and never developed to normal maturity.

Ralph Waldo Emerson was born, then, of the intellectual aristocracy of New England. He was one of the clerical and literary élite. Behind him, and he believed strongly in

9

race and lineage, was a long line of ministers, preachers, and scholars. His father had been a writer and editor as well as the minister of Boston's leading church. His step-grandfather, Dr. Ezra Ripley, for his grandmother had remarried when she was left a widow, was the minister of Concord. Various uncles were ministers or teachers near by.

The Emerson family moved by right of birth among the intellectual and cultured of Boston and its surrounding cities and towns. They knew, naturally, the other well-educated and often affluent families who, like them, had been established as the leaders of New England for almost two centuries. The Emerson name and associations would open academic and professional doors to them at which many, less fortunately born, could never have the opportunity to knock.

Yet, financially, life was difficult for the Emerson boys and their widowed mother, even though the First Church was generous. It continued the Reverend William Emerson's salary for six months after his death. It then allowed the widow five hundred dollars a year for seven years, a considerable sum of money in the second decade of the nineteenth century. The family were allowed to continue living in the church parsonage for three years.

The parsonage in which Ralph Waldo Emerson was born was on Sumner Street in Boston. The parsonage in which he grew up after 1808 was in the city of Boston too, but its surroundings were more countrylike than urban. The house, with its own gardens and orchards, stood well back from the street in a corner of Chauncy Place. There were bordering rows of elms and Lombardy poplars. The section was one of spacious estates, each with its own wide lawns and gardens. Near by was a two-acre pasture. The sound of cowbells was a familiar one during Emerson's childhood.

Ruth Haskins Emerson, very devout, serene of countenance, with dark liquid eyes and a musical voice, was determined that her fatherless sons should have the best possible education. Even more determined was the boys' diminutive aunt, their father's sister, who lived with them much of the time during this period. Mary Moody Emerson was to have a strong and lasting influence on the life of her nephew.

Before he left Concord to join the Continental Army, her father had taken his infant daughter to his mother's home in Malden and asked her to care for the child until his return. After his death and her mother's remarriage, tiny Mary Moody Emerson remained with her grandmother. Later, she lived on a farm with an uncle who, Emerson said, was shiftless. His farm did not prosper.

The small girl had not only to work about the house and farm, but also to keep an eye out for the sheriff, who might well appear to arrest the uncle for debt or confiscate the family spoons. Another aunt, who was insane, was brought into the household, and caring for her was added to the girl's chores. Mary Moody Emerson grew up among these old people with no companions of her own age. Religious books, which she read avidly, were her only companions. She read, reread, and reveled in a torn copy of *Paradise Lost* which had neither cover nor title page. Not until years later did she find out that John Milton had written it.

The promise that the farm would be left to her was kept. It was sold and its purchase price put into another farm in Maine, where Mary Emerson lived for many years as a boarder in the home of a sister. Again, she was much alone with nature and her religious books. At one point she refused, probably on religious grounds, to marry a man whom Emerson described as having talent, education, and social position. Throughout the years it was her habit to visit the homes of brothers and sisters when illness or death made her feel she could be of help. It was so she came to stay in the Chauncy Place parsonage.

11

This spinster aunt, deeply read, a capable writer, was tart and difficult. All of four feet three inches high, she was as independent as she pleased in her manners and opinions, and she pleased to be very independent. She adored her nephews. She declared they were born to be educated. They would be scholars and thinkers, orators, men brilliant and admired in the world of Boston. These were the goals she set for them. She urged them on furiously. Scorn trifles, she demanded. Lift your aims. Do what you are afraid to do.

Mary Moody Emerson was not too comfortable to have around for long. She knew this and was proud of it. For years she slept in a bed shaped like a coffin. She made herself a burial shroud and wore it as a nightgown or a day gown. Sometimes, a cloak over it, she rode horseback in the same shroud. When it wore out, she had another made. She carried one with her in all her travels. She was always prepared for death, but she lived to the full.

"She had the misfortune," Emerson wrote in his biographical essay about her, "of spinning with a greater velocity than any of the other tops." She was impatient of tops that spun more slowly and contemptuous of those that toppled. She delighted in disconcerting with abrupt remarks. She expressed her unorthodox opinions forcefully and, when she chose, rudely. She was a goad but an inspiration to her nephews. Emerson never ceased to acknowledge his indebtedness to Mary Moody Emerson. "She gave high counsels. It was the privilege of certain boys to have this immeasurably high standard indicated to their childhood; a blessing which nothing else in education could supply."

Emerson started school when he was two years old. He went to a Miss Nancy Dickson's Dame School. He was not yet three years old when his father complained that his son still did not read very well. From this earliest school, Emerson went on to a grammar school run by a severe master, Lawson Lyons. He entered the Boston Latin School when he was ten.

He was allowed out of school an hour early each day so that he could also attend Mr. Webb's writing school on the other side of Boston Common. Indignantly and rather amusingly defending his father against the charge of an English biographer that, even as a small boy, Emerson was always correctly behaved, Dr. Edward Emerson says that Ralph Waldo often played truant from Mr. Webb's to play on the Common.

Like other Boston boys, Emerson knew the names of the city's fire engines—"Extinguisher," "Cataract," "Dispatch," and the rest—and probably chased after them to fires when he could. Sometimes in warm weather he went swimming after school. In Boston, where most winters the snow is plentiful and sledding is a standard winter sport, Emerson never had a sled. One reason was that he would not have dared use it for fear of the city's boy gangs. The Round Pointers and the South Enders deployed past the Emerson parsonage on their way to the Common, where they fought the "rumbles" of the time with the West Enders. Emerson's mother had warned him against these ruffians of the streets. The boy used to hang over their garden gate hoping for a sight of them.

There was play, but not much, for the Emerson boys. They were too busy helping with the household chores and, spurred on by the urging of their aunt, at their books. They needed little urging. The brothers reveled in history, fiction, and always poetry. On the Puritan Sabbath, which still prevailed, there was, of course, no play at all. Probably all but the Bible and religious books were forbidden. Emerson used to amuse himself by repeating ordinary words over and over until they had lost their meaning. Church offered one delight. He enjoyed the sneezing and

13

nose-blowing and wheezing of the older men. "They would snort and roar through their noses like the lowing of an ox," he said.

William Henry Furness, a schoolmate and life-long friend who became a Philadelphia minister, says that Emerson played little as a child and boy. It was usually books instead. Furness remembered Emerson's writing away in his copybook at Mr. Webb's, his tongue working up and down as he labored with his pen. Another schoolmate, Rufus Dawes, said Emerson was a spiritual-looking boy in blue nankeen. Nankeen was a cheap, tough cotton cloth from China, the common summer wear of boys at that time. It was the kind of serviceable clothing the Emerson boys, of necessity, had to wear.

Clothing was not plentiful with them. At one period, and in frigid New England, William and Ralph Waldo had only one overcoat between them. Their schoolmates amused themselves by taunting them about it: "Whose turn to wear the coat today?"

Emerson was not overly popular with the other boys at school. He was a little too aloof. As he was to do all his life, he kept his distance. Probably his fellows resented what one told Oliver Wendell Holmes many years later: Emerson seemed "to dwell apart as if in a tower, from which he looked upon everything through a loophole of his own." Emerson liked his studies—except mathematics, which he never mastered—and did fairly well at them, but he thought he profited more from random reading of his own.

He was at the Boston Latin School during the War of 1812. When a British squadron attacked Boston Harbor, Bostonians were able to watch the naval engagement from their rooftops. Emerson and some of the other boys from the school volunteered to do some shoveling on the breast-works on Noddle's Island, but he could not remember that they actually did any work. Instead, already writing and declaiming rhymes, he wrote patriotic verses in honor of the United States frigates which were fighting the war.

When their extended three-year tenancy was up, and a Mr. Frothingham was installed as minister of the First Church and needed the parsonage, Mrs. Emerson moved with her five small boys to a house on Atkinson Street, then to another on Beacon Hill, where she took in boarders to help support her family. The home life they knew was austere. The Emersons' genteel poverty did not admit of the luxuries and sometimes even of the ordinary comforts. As one biographer puts it, the boys were staunch because they had to be. Once, when they were actually in need of food, their aunt cheered them up with tales of heroic endurance. This did not fill their stomachs, but it was about all she could do for them, and the boys were heroes. They had no choice.

By the end of 1814 the financial condition of the family was so low that Dr. Ezra Ripley took his stepson's widow and her sons home to live with him in the Old Manse in Concord, which had been built by Emerson's grandfather before he went to the Revolutionary War. William, the eldest son, was now a Harvard freshman at thirteen. Edward, Charles, and Ralph Waldo attended the Concord school.

Coming to know the fields and woods of his ancestors for the first time, Emerson was entranced by nature, whose influence on him was to be so important throughout his life. The brothers, as aliens from the city, had some quarrels with their Concord schoolfellows, but they were happy in the manse beside the Concord River. When Emerson was sent to Deacon White's store in the village, the clerk would set him up on a barrel and have him recite poetry: Campbell's "Glenara," Milton, or stirring passages from the kind of poetry schoolboys of the nineteenth century were taught to declaim.

By 1815 the family was back in Boston. This time Mrs.

Emerson and his brothers went to school in Boston and Concord.

Emerson was lent a house near the Athenaeum while its owner was in Europe. In return, she provided board and room for his wife and children. Dr. Ripley sent a cow back with the family from Concord. It became one of Emerson's daily chores to drive it back and forth around the Common to a pasture on Carver Street.

Frugality and industry, plain living and hard work, dreams, ambitions, resolves: this was more than ever the Emerson diet now. William was working hard at college both to succeed for himself and to help his brothers. As the oldest son, he felt responsible. Ralph Waldo, Edward, and Charles were all preparing for Harvard. The childlike Robert was incapable of being educated at either school or college. The family was close-knit in its determination. The brothers were their own companions and competitors. Their mother was a steady, guiding influence. Aunt Mary, strong in the old Puritan beliefs, helped tug and haul at the wagons she had insisted they hitch to the brightest stars she could imagine.

It is easy to picture the proud and wistful small boy, rather lonely as he walked the pleasant Boston streets near his home or chivvied their cow along. He was thin and growing tall. His hair was brown. His eyes were as blue as the sky. His imagination was fired by the tales of great men and heroic deeds which he and his brothers read. Deprivation had fired the appetites of them all to excel. Knowledge of his family's proud history in New England and the eminence of his scholarly ministerial forebears, as well as the admonitions of his tireless aunt, further fired his ambition.

He reveled in the sight of trees, shrubs, and flowers which made him think of the fields and pine woods of Concord. He delighted in the sky, in the shapes of clouds, in light and shadow. On cold days, dressed not quite warmly enough, he leaned into the northwest wind on his way to and from school. He knew he was Ralph Waldo

17

Emerson. He felt a little apart. At the same time, he felt a part of all he saw and heard, the trees and the grass, the snow and ice, other people on the street, Boston, the budding United States, the whole universe.

Men and cities, mountains and plains, the ancient cities of Greece and Rome, the stars at night, all fascinated him. That was why it was hard to fasten his attention on mathematics or the argument of some preacher whom he heard on Sunday or whose sermons he was made to read in school.

Soon, like his brother William, he would be at Harvard. Emerson both looked forward to college and dreaded it. It would be a step forward in his career. William's stories of his wise and learned professors and of friends in his class were exciting. Yet he would be leaving home for the first time, and he was not always certain that he could measure up to all that was expected of him. His younger brother Edward and the still younger Charles did better at school than he. People said they were the brilliant ones who would become the orators and poets.

Loans from friends, scholarships, occasional prizes of small sums of money for recitations or poems by one or another of the brothers all helped. In 1817, when he was fourteen years old, Emerson entered Harvard College.

As "President's Freshman," he ran errands for Harvard President John Thornton Kirkland and in return received his room in the house of the round-faced, smiling president. He waited on table in the Harvard Commons and earned his board that way. He was private tutor to the president's nephew, Samuel Kirkland Lothrop. Lothrop, who became a minister, remembered that the fourteen-year-old freshman was just what he was afterward, "kindly, affable, but self-contained."

Slender, delicate, younger than most of his classmates, Emerson excelled in Greek under Edward Everett, whom he liked, and worked hard on his English compositions for

18

Professor Edward Tyrrel Channing, but unlike his brothers, he was far from being an outstanding student. Though he read widely on his own—Shakespeare, Swift, Locke, the early English dramatists—he did not do well in his assigned subjects. In time he joined the Conventicle and became a member and secretary of the Pythologian, social, and literary clubs, but his home life had hardly prepared him for social success. He tried to be convivial, but, as he wrote in the journal which he started in 1820, he was not too successful at it.

Once he wrote, "I drank a good deal of wine (for me) with the wish to raise my spirits to the pitch of good fellowship, but wine produced its old effect. I grew graver with every glass." The Malaga wine came from Warfield's, a Cambridge grocer's, and Emerson said it was most delicious though it did little to raise what he called his animal spirits. He lamented all through life that his animal spirits were low. He never knew the excess of energy that comes from vibrant health.

His spare and Spartan upbringing was not conducive to conviviality. He was not and did not want to be a big man on campus. Both geographically and emotionally, his home was close to him. When he won five dollars for a prize declamation, for Emerson had a natural gift for the platform from the beginning, he sent the money home to his mother, hoping she would buy a shawl with it. It went for necessities instead. He wrote a two-hundred-word poem for the Pythologian and a long college paper on "The Character of Socrates." During college vacations, as William had done before him and Edward and Charles would do later, he acted as usher in his uncle Samuel Ripley's school in Waltham.

His college mates, who had already decided on their professions or had the decision made for them, had an easier and less worrisome time. They knew where they were going and could direct their energies toward their limited goals. Emerson's mind and imagination ranged too wide and far for that. He wanted to be more than just a doctor, a lawyer, a minister. He was in love with words. The stirring expression of poetic thought intoxicated him where Warfield's wine depressed.

Emerson just managed to stay in the top half of his class. Neither his college mates nor his professors saw in him any indication of future greatness. Alone in the midst of the crowd, he was feeling his way. He burned with ambition to achieve, but to achieve he did not yet know what. He fretted at his seeming delay in accomplishing anything he valued. His moods ran the scale from bright hope to black despondency. He worried about his chances and his short-comings.

"I find myself often idle, vagrant, stupid and hollow," he wrote in his journal, October 25, 1820, when he was seventeen. "This is somewhat appalling and, if I do not discipline myself with diligent care, I shall suffer severely from remorse and the sense of inferiority hereafter." Others about him seemed busy and destined for greatness. He felt he was not competing successfully. He felt, as often in later life, that he needed greater stimulus. "I need excitement," he wrote.

By "excitement," Emerson meant something which would stir him to eloquence, to poetic achievement. He resolved to make himself thoroughly familiar with Greek and Greek history. He deplored his failure at mathematics and hoped he could compensate by his abilities with his pen. He was reading Francis Bacon and Ben Jonson, not so much for what they said as how they said it, trying to find out how they wrote effectively so that he might do so himself.

His journal, even more than his books, was becoming Emerson's intimate companion. It was to serve him all his life as his primary means of expression. It was a place to put down all the thoughts he could not yet express to others or in any other form. He intended his journal to be a record of new thoughts, of old ideas, even of stray fancies. It would be his memory and serve him later as a mine or reservoir of material for writing, for sermons, for essays, for poetry—for just what he was not yet sure.

During his junior year in Harvard, Emerson lived in Hollis Hall with a classmate from South Carolina, John G. K. Jourdin. In his senior year he roomed with his younger brother Edward, who was a freshman. Handsome, popular, brilliant Edward, already a leader in his class, was to be a far greater success at Harvard than Ralph Waldo. He got up at five o'clock every morning to write his own themes, then themes for other less gifted students, who paid him fifty cents each. He would graduate from Harvard far and away the head of his class.

Emerson did not. He graduated in 1821, still barely in the upper half of his class. He was class poet, but the honor became his only after seven others, evidently thought then to be better poets, had refused it. In a college graduation exercise he played the part of John Knox, the Scottish reform preacher of the sixteenth century.

Emerson's ambition when he graduated was to be a professor of rhetoric and elocution, a teacher of writing and speaking, but no one offered him such a job.

2

On his graduation from Harvard a few years earlier, William Emerson had gone to teach in a high school in Kennebunk, Maine. The year before Emerson's graduation, he had come home and opened a girls' school in his mother's house. The school was going well. William offered his brother a job as his assistant, and, for lack of better opportunity, Emerson took it.

William was twenty and Ralph, or Waldo, as he began to call himself after he left college, was eighteen. Only a few years older than their students, the brothers found it necessary to make up for their youthfulness by great dignity and reserve. In private they teased each other about their finishing school for young ladies of the first families of Boston, but in the classroom their dignity was awesome. Undoubtedly, Emerson had, too, the quiet charm, the gentle fascination that his presence exerted on others throughout his life. There was no nervousness behind his reserve. He felt sure always of what he knew and taught.

At the same time he felt shy and awkward in his first job. The girls saw to that. Knowing that he was still too young to vote, they would beg for a holiday on election days, saying they knew he needed the time free to go to cast his ballot.

Emerson disliked teaching. He took his work seriously, but resented what he found its dull and uninspiring routine. "I have never expected," he wrote in his journal, "success in my present employment. My scholars are carefully instructed, my money is faithfully earned, but the instructor is little wiser, and the duties were never congenial with my disposition."

He wanted success. The word was often in his mind and the idea appears often in his journal. It was not to be a vulgar success, he and his Aunt Mary agreed, but fame in the realm of thought and spirit. "Lifting the truncheon against the fair-haired daughters of this raw city," as he described his teaching on another occasion, did not seem to him the way to go about obtaining it.

In the spring of 1824 the Emersons moved again, this time to Canterbury, then a wooded district of Roxbury some four miles outside the limits of the city of Boston. The family rented a farmhouse on Canterbury Lane, which was called Dark Lane because of the dense shadow cast by the tall trees or, ironically, Light Lane. Town wits called it Featherbed Lane because of the rough pebbled road.

Whatever it was called, this was the country, and Emerson, ever sensitive to rural scenes, loved it. Stretched out under some pines in Canterbury in April 1824, he expressed some of his melancholy and frustration as well as his relief in the first of what were to become his better-known poems. It was not his first poem; he had been writing verse since boyhood. But it is the first which later he included in his published verse. Youthful sadness after the manner of Thomas Gray's "Elegy Written in a Country Church-yard" is stiffened by Emerson's proud defiance.

23

Good-bye, proud world! I'm going home:
Thou art not my friend, and I'm not thine.
Long through thy weary crowds I roam;
A river-ark on the ocean brine,
Long I've been tossed like the driven foam;
But now, proud world! I'm going home.

Good-bye to Flattery's fawning face;
To Grandeur with his wise grimace;
To upstart Wealth's averted eye;
To supple Office, low and high;
To crowded halls, to court and street;
To frozen hearts and hasting feet;
To those who go, and those who come;
Good-bye, proud world! I'm going home.

I am going to my own hearth-stone,
Bosomed in yon green fields alone,—
A secret nook in a pleasant land,
Whose groves the frolic fairies planned;
Where arches green, the livelong day,
Echo the blackbird's roundelay,
And vulgar feet have never trod
A spot that is sacred to thought and God. . . .

Expressing himself in poetry must have pleased Emerson. That he could write a poem at all in those days delighted him. He could never write verse on demand or through an effort of will. He needed the right mood, a calm happiness, for his emotions, thoughts, words, and music to fall into place and fuse in poetry. As a poet, and by his own admission, Emerson was always dependent on "inspiration."

He was reading widely, writing busily in his journal, trying to find a vocation and himself. Most of the time it seemed to him he was making no headway at all in any direction. Living in the country was an improvement, but it was merely an external circumstance, a palliation of his unease. It helped, but it did not cure.

Emerson was suffering from a typical after-college let-down. In college, where he had lived with ideas and dreams, stirred by his studies of ancient civilizations, thrilled by the older English poets, aroused by the teeming life in Shakespeare, drunk with the sound of words and the beauty of language, everything had seemed possible. In comparison, teaching school was prosaic and mundane. This hardly accorded with his dream of moving men by his eloquence. He was not even sure now that this was what he wanted most to do. He knew only that he wanted greater challenge than a room full of obedient society girls in his mother's parlor. He felt he had been born for victory, but victory at what? This was not even a skirmish. It was just dull.

As in college, his moods shot up and plummeted down. He was dejected, then rebellious. He saw no reason, he told himself sharply, why he should bow his head to any man or cringe to anyone. He had not much cause, he told himself in his journal, to thank his alma mater. He had not often felt the flattery of success while at Harvard. Often he had felt unhappy at his fate and particularly with his own efforts. Yet at college he had known his brightest thoughts. He had felt sentiment sometimes. He had felt poetic. Now, he missed the society of his fellows. He missed the walks he used to take. He felt happy when, the February after his graduation, he went back to Cambridge on a visit.

By May he was depressed again. He would be nineteen years old in a few days. "Has any other educated person lived so many years and lost so many days?" He did not like himself much. He was too cold. He was too cautious. He was too selfish. He wanted to feel romantic, but he did not know how. "I have not the kind affections of a pigeon."

Twelve months later, ambitions still unsatisfied, he bemoaned the passing of another year. He was almost twenty, yet he still had achieved neither fame nor fortune. Alone

25

one Sunday evening in late March of 1823, he wrote in his journal: "One youth among the multitudes of mankind, one grain of sand on the seashore, unknown in the midst of my contemporaries, I am hastening to put on the manly robe. From childhood the names of the great have ever resounded in my ear, and it is impossible that I should be indifferent to the rank which I must take in the innumerable assembly of men. . . ." Ambition was more than unsatisfied. It gnawed at him.

Emerson tried to comfort himself by writing long, affected, consciously lighthearted letters to some of his college friends. They seem labored. The flippancy sounds strained. Lonely, unhappy because he expected so much of himself so soon, Emerson appears rather a prig in these young, soon-after-college years.

With the school well established, William left it in Waldo's charge and sailed for Germany to study for the ministry. The eldest son had been emancipated. The family was no longer in want. Edward graduated from Harvard this year, 1824, with top honors. Everyone prophesied a splendid future for the most resplendent of the Emerson boys. He started a school in Roxbury as his first step to the stars. Charles entered Harvard as Edward left.

Doggedly, Emerson kept on with his teaching. In the privacy of his room he was striving to write. Moral beauty, he decided, was the reality. Physical beauty soon perishes. Moral beauty endures forever. Wordsworth stood for moral beauty. So earlier had Jonathan Edwards, greatest of the Puritan divines. The romantic poet and the stern Calvinist shared a belief that became Emerson's too. Things unseen are eternal, the Bible had said.

The girls in his school tried to flatter him by pretending an interest in any book or author they knew he was reading. Emerson may have felt flattered, but he was not convinced that teaching them did him any more good than it did them. On February 8, 1825, he closed the school. The next day he entered the middle class of the Harvard Divinity School to study for the Unitarian ministry.

It was a deliberate decision, coldly made. Emerson seems to have felt no "call" to the ministry. It was his ancestral profession. He had saved between two and three thousand dollars from his teaching. Financially it was possible for him to continue his studies. "I deliberately dedicate my time, my talents, and my hopes to the Church," was the decision he entered in his journal. It sounds as if it cost him an effort of will.

As he neared his twenty-first birthday, Emerson once again took stock of himself. This time, he said, he would not pretend, even to himself, that his abilities were as great as his ambition. He knew he had a strong imagination, consequently a keen love for the beauties of poetry. He was immoderately fond of writing. His reasoning powers, he felt, were weaker. The kind of preaching then in fashion demanded less of thought and reason than of imagination for success. Emerson felt he had the imagination and the literary talent to become a successful minister. Thus, practically, he justified his choice of profession.

Emerson had what he considered an unfortunate propensity to laugh too much. He would have to check it and appear more dignified. He was often ill at ease in company. Fear of somehow offending or of showing disrespect made it difficult for him to pay full attention to a conversation. As a result, he came out poorly among the others present, when he wished painfully to be first.

Sometimes, he thought, he criticized too much. Sometimes he praised too much. He argued weakly. He knew he would have made a poor lawyer. "But in Divinity," he wrote, April 18, 1824, "I hope to thrive. I inherit from my sire a formality of manner and speech, but I derive from him, or his patriotic parent, a passionate love for the strains of eloquence."

It was a frank, cold, and fairly accurate appraisal of

himself that Emerson made. He chose the Unitarian ministry for reasons of sound common sense, not from religious zeal. As a minister he could advance more rapidly toward the goals he desired. The Unitarian was the most fashionable and socially acceptable of the Protestant denominations in Boston and Cambridge at the time. It was the church of the educated and well-to-do. Emerson planned to do well in it.

Another circumstance may well have contributed to Emerson's decision. After two years of study in Göttingen, William found himself troubled by religious doubts. He abandoned his plans for the Church and returned home to begin the study of law. No doubt, both their mother and the redoubtable Aunt Mary were grieved. It was up to Ralph Waldo Emerson now.

Just a month after he entered Divinity School, Emerson fell ill. It was impossible for him to continue his studies. The hard years of his boyhood, the strain of college on meager funds, three years of work at what he disliked, and thwarted ambition may have helped bring on his collapse.

Emerson's eyes gave out. Rheumatism brought on a lameness in one hip. He felt weak and unwell. It is possible that some of his illness was brought on by what today would be called "psychosomatic" causes. Emerson's psyche, his spirit, may well have rebelled against the deliberate decision of his will to enter the ministry. At heart he did not believe in or wish to do what he was doing.

In an attempt to recover his health, he went to the farm of an uncle in Newton and worked there as a laborer. The next fall, still with weak eyes and a lame hip, he took a school in Chelmsford where the mentally retarded brother, Robert Bulkeley, lived on a farm. From Chelmsford, Emerson returned to Roxbury to carry on the school which Edward had started. Edward's health, too, had given way, and he had sailed for the Mediterranean. Later in 1826,

Emerson took pupils in a room of the house which his mother had now rented in Cambridge. For a time he taught in Boston, where one of his pupils was Richard Henry Dana, to become famous later as the author of *Two Years Before the Mast*.

At odd times and as he could, Emerson continued his theological studies. On October 10, 1826, he was licensed —"approbated"—to preach by the Middlesex County Association of Ministers.

Undoubtedly this board took into consideration the Emerson family name, the fame which Emersons had achieved as preachers, the difficulties under which Emerson had conducted his desultory studies. If they had examined him, Emerson said later, he doubted that they would have passed him and allowed him to preach.

Almost immediately, Emerson was ill again, this time more seriously. The eye weakness and the lameness continued. Now there had been for some time a painful stricture in his chest. Emerson was threatened with the family malady of tuberculosis. The doctors insisted that he journey south. His uncle, the Reverend Samuel Ripley, provided the funds, and, on Christmas Day, 1826, Emerson set sail from Boston in the brig *Clematis*. Twelve days later he landed in Charleston, South Carolina. When Charleston's winter proved too cold and damp, he embarked again, and this time landed in St. Augustine, Florida.

Used only to bare and bleak New England, Emerson found St. Augustine—which had been founded in 1565 and thus was the better part of a century older than Boston —a queer place indeed. There were about eleven or twelve hundred people: invalids, public officials, and Minorcan Spaniards. They did nothing, or so little that it seemed nothing to Emerson. Florida had been taken over by the United States only five years before. Public offices were now held by Americans. The Spanish kept billiard tables or, when that proved too strenuous, sent their slaves to dig oysters in the mud or bring back fish from the shore. A report that a man was seen working in the city's public square brought everybody out to watch him. There were a few orange groves, but they were ill-tended. One Negro, Emerson saw, gave his sluggish attention to each five or six hundred trees.

Yet the air and sky were delicious. Emerson strolled on the beach. Solo, he played a kind of impromptu golf, driving a green orange over the hard sands of the shore with a stick. He read and wrote a little. Halfheartedly, he outlined sermons which he felt he might never preach.

He saw the iron gibbets, man-shaped cages in which the Spanish used to hang criminals in trees to perish. Some of the gibbets which had been dug up were full of old bones. The local priest had been arrested for debt, but, generously, his creditors allowed him out of jail to conduct church services. Emerson went to a different kind of service himself and described it in his journal.

The St. Augustine branch of the Bible Society held a meeting at the government house. The society's treasurer, who was also district marshal, had forgetfully arranged for a slave auction in the same place at the same time. "One ear therefore heard the glad tidings of great joy, whilst the other was regaled with 'Going, gentlemen, going!' and, almost without changing our position we might aid in sending the Scriptures into Africa, or bid for 'four children without the mother' who had been kidnapped therefrom."

While in Florida, Emerson met a man with whose force and abilities he was impressed. He made friends with Achille Murat, son of Joachim Murat, Marshal of France, and a nephew of Napoleon. This was hardly the kind of man Emerson had known in Harvard College or met at Divinity School. Emerson found Murat "a philosopher, a scholar, a man of the world; very skeptical, but very candid, and an ardent lover of the truth." When he left St. Augustine, Emerson visited Murat at his Tallahassee plantation.

Emerson met Achille Murat when he went to St. Augustine.

31

Together the two men sailed back to Charleston. Murat's company made the sea voyage endurable.

Emerson had preached his first sermon in Waltham, taking as his subject the remark of a Methodist farm laborer with whom he had worked in Newton. This man had told Emerson that all prayers are answered. They had better be careful, then, Emerson told the first congregation he addressed as a minister, what they prayed for.

In Charleston, Emerson preached again. This time he talked on a favorite conviction that was to become one of his basic doctrines. He urged his listeners to be independent in their judgments and to act without regard to custom. He told them not to try to conform to the opinions of others and not to worry about the influence of their examples. They were to act from the simplest motives and in accord with the dictates of their own minds and hearts. It was self-reliance he preached.

The stricture in his chest somewhat relieved by the soft Florida air, Emerson preached his way back to Boston. He delivered sermons in Charleston, Washington, Philadelphia, and New York. From Alexandria, Virginia, he wrote his Aunt Mary: "I am not sure that I am a jot better or worse than when I left home in November. Only in this, that I preached Sunday morning in Washington without any pain or inconvenience." He signed himself "your poor blinded but very affectionate nephew."

Once home, though still far from completely well, he continued for another year as a theological student, supplying the pulpits of ministerial relatives and friends but not seeking a church of his own. That he avoided. Several times he refused to preach as a candidate for a vacant pulpit. Something held him back.

While its minister was away, he preached at what had been his father's church, the First Church in Boston. He preached in Northampton, where Jonathan Edwards had been minister a hundred years before. He preached for a ministerial relative, Dr. Dewey, in New Bedford. He read the English and Scottish reviews, the literary magazines. He began to read Emanuel Swedenborg. Not Harvard but Samson Reed, a Boston druggist, introduced him to the writings of the Swedish mystic. He went on a visit to a relative in Concord, New Hampshire.

In February 1828, Emerson wrote William that he had refused still another offer to preach as a candidate for a vacant pulpit. He had begged off on the excuse of not feeling well enough. How, he wondered, though he did not sound seriously concerned, was he to get his bread? He was living, he told William, like a man treading on eggs. Life and death were battling over him, and he was not sure which would win. He never wrote, he said, when he could walk or, especially, when he could laugh. Though he always tried to check his own tendency to laugh, considering it unseemly, Emerson sought the society of laughers in those days.

In another letter he warned William not to work too hard. All the Emersons, he proclaimed, overdid themselves. He was taking as much exercise as his hip would bear. Walking was more than mere exercise for Emerson. It was almost a way of life. From it he drew sustenance for his spirit as well as muscle tone for his legs.

"It is a peculiarity of humor in me," Emerson once wrote, "my strong propensity for strolling. I deliberately shut up my books in a cloudy July noon, put on my old clothes and old hat, and slink away to the whortleberry bushes, and slip with the greatest satisfaction into a little cow-path, where I am sure I can defy observation. This point gained, I solace myself for hours with picking blueberries and other trash of the woods, far from fame behind the birch trees. I seldom enjoy hours as I do these. I remember them in winter; I expect them in spring. I do not know a creature that I think has the same humor or would think it respectable."

Emerson's warning to William might well have been heeded by the feverishly striving Edward. On his return from the Mediterranean, Edward had rushed into employment after employment in frantic pursuit of early success. A brilliant student, he was also a brilliant teacher. He was a private tutor. A favorite in society, notable for his striking appearance and his forceful and persuasive speech, he became Daniel Webster's confidential clerk. When he had to be away, Webster even left his children in Edward's charge, saying he knew Edward could do a better job of caring for them than he could do himself. While he studied law as Webster's clerk, Edward read three hours a day to the nearly blind Harvard historian William Hickling Prescott. In his spare time he catalogued books for the Boston Athenaeum.

Ill anew, Edward was at the Old Manse in Concord in the early summer of 1828 when he grew much worse. Fainting fits were followed by delirium and delirium by insanity. "Yesterday we brought Edward down to Charlestown," Emerson wrote William, July 3, 1828. "His frenzy took all forms; but what's the use of relating them? There he lay—Edward, the admired, learned, eloquent, striving boy—a maniac."

Emerson grieved for his younger brother. This was the ruin of all Edward's towering hopes. Emerson was almost glad now for what he called his own slowness, embarrassed manner, and sometimes flippant speech. It was a safeguard against the madness which had assailed Edward. An egoist, as most great men and all serious writers are, Emerson could not help contrasting himself with his more socially gifted brother.

He himself, he thought, had so much *silliness*—he underlined the word in his journal—in his makeup that he was probably safe from madness. He laughed too easily; he blushed too easily. He looked ill-tempered when he did not wish to. Edward had always shown great facial control.

Emerson showed too easily what he thought. He thought that he often injured his chances with other people by the way he looked and acted. His judgments of himself were, of course, exaggerated, but he was a self-conscious and ambitious young man burning to make his way in the world and establish his place in it.

Edward recovered his reason but not his health. Abandoning all of his activities and most of his hopes, he sailed for the West Indies where, to support himself, he took a job as a clerk.

As Edward's star tumbled, Emerson's rose rocketlike. The prospects of the half-ill, often depressed, and seemingly often bewildered Ralph Waldo Emerson shot up fast and high. His fortunes, both personal and professional, changed with dramatic suddenness.

In Concord, New Hampshire, Emerson had met Ellen Louisa Tucker, beautiful seventeen-year-old daughter of a rich Boston merchant whose widow had married Colonel William Austen Kent. Colonel Kent was a wealthy bank and insurance-company director who also controlled a trading company with boats plying the Merrimac River and the Middlesex Canal. Emerson, who preached at the Unitarian church which Colonel Kent had helped form, had been entertained at the Kent mansion, where both President Monroe and Lafayette had been entertained before him and where Daniel Webster was a frequent guest.

It was a gay and fashionable household of girls. There were Margaret and Paulina, Ellen's sisters, and Mary Jane and Rebecca, Colonel Kent's daughters by a previous marriage. There was music and parties. There were riding horses, a spaniel (named Byron), squirrels, a canary, even white mice among the household pets. Emerson fell deeply in love with Ellen Tucker, whose health was delicate but thought to be improving, though one sister and an older brother had already died of tuberculosis. Ellen, who seemed much better after a long carriage trip through New Hamp-

35

shire and Massachusetts in the summer of 1828, was equally in love with the twenty-five-year-old minister. Their engagement was announced in December.

Emerson wrote a score of romantic poems to his beloved. She wrote him rapturous letters, gay, often witty, filled with girlish happiness. She made light of her illness, wrote frankly and eagerly of their love. These letters still exist and were published in 1962. It is thought that Emerson may have destroyed his to Ellen, for none have been found. Emerson was ecstatically happy—and his brothers noted appreciatively that Ellen was not only beautiful, sensible, and religious, but also rich.

Professional opportunity came at almost the same time. Emerson was invited to become assistant to the Reverend Henry Ware, Jr., minister of the Second Church in Boston. This was the famous old North Church where the signal lanterns were displayed for Paul Revere on the night of his famous ride. Increase Mather had become its Puritan head in 1664. His son, Cotton Mather (a leader in the Salem witchcraft trials), had preached there until 1723. This was not a post for an ambitious young man to turn down. Emerson substituted in its pulpit while Ware was ill. On March 11, 1829, he was ordained assistant pastor of the Second Church. A few weeks later Ware resigned to travel in Europe for his health, and Ralph Waldo Emerson became pastor of the Second Church. He and Ellen Tucker were married at the Kent mansion in September.

Emerson was twenty-six years of age. Despite what he called "my unpleasing boyhood," despite fretting at hindrances, he had, in the words of his friend and official biographer, James Elliot Cabot, "promptly and easily reached a position that might satisfy all of his aspirations; he was the head of an honored church; he was married to a wife who was 'a bright revelation to me of the best nature of woman'; he was able to provide a comfortable home for his mother and a gathering place for the brothers . . ."

Ill health forgotten in his new happiness, Emerson thrilled the staid congregation of the Second Church by his unaffected sincerity in the pulpit. He spoke simply. He made no attempt to speak with the artificial eloquence he had once admired. He spoke instead with quiet conviction of the simple spiritual truths he saw as the heart of all religious feeling.

His tall, slender presence, his serene countenance, the high forehead, the aquiline profile, and the striking sky-blue eyes affected even those who paid little attention to the very liberal gospel that Emerson preached. Many spoke then, as many were to do later in his life, of his "angelic" presence. His charm, his musical voice and gentle manner, seem to have had an almost hypnotic effect from the pulpit or the platform.

Emerson was a preacher, not a pastor tending his flock. He disliked such ministerial duties as calling on the sick and dying. He saw himself as the inspirer of minds and souls, not as a comforter for physical miseries, and he felt clumsy and ill at ease when he attempted pastoral visits. One sharp-spoken old man on whom he called told him he did not know his business very well, but most were too pleased with his voice and pulpit manner to care.

Emerson was happy fulfilling the duties of his churchly office, and he was happy in his home life. His mother kept house for him and his fragile bride in a house which they took on Chardon Street in Boston. On Sundays, in a day when most worshippers walked to church, Ellen Emerson rode proudly to the Second Church in her carriage to see and hear her admired young husband.

She did not go often. Ellen's health, instead of improving, grew worse. It became so bad that during the first winter of his ministry at the Second Church, Emerson was forced to take his wife south and leave her with her family in a milder climate. There was a brief respite that was only a respite. Ellen Tucker Emerson died of tuberculosis on

37

February 8, 1831. She and Emerson had been married a year and a half.

Emerson was broken at her death. He wrote in his journal of the wasted, empty days, of his apathy. Daily he visited Ellen's grave and tried to lose himself in his work. The apathy persisted, though he knew it would go in time. Emerson never forgot his first love. He wrote tenderly of Ellen in his journal many years later.

With Ellen gone, the Church became more difficult for him. Emerson's religious impulse was deep; almost as deep-seated was his growing dislike for the forms of religious worship. It was the spirit that mattered, not creeds or ceremonies. Less than six months after Ellen's death he wrote in his journal, "I suppose it is not wise, not being natural, to belong to any religious party. In the Bible you are not directed to be a Unitarian, or a Calvinist or an Episcopalian. Now if a man is wise, . . . he will say to himself, I am not a member of that or of any party. I am God's child, a disciple of Christ, or, in the eye of God, a fellow disciple with Christ."

In New Bedford he had been impressed by the Quakers he met and had found himself in sympathy with their complete lack of set forms of worship. Many years later, when someone asked him about his religion, he said he supposed he was more of a Quaker than anything else, though he never professed to be a Friend.

Emerson's tone became sharper. "It is the best part of the man, I sometimes think," he wrote in January 1832, "that revolts most against his being a minister." Six months later he commented unhappily, "I have sometimes thought that, in order to be a good minister, it was necessary to leave the ministry. . . . In an altered age, we worship in the dead forms of our forefathers."

Purpose was forming in Emerson, character hardening. Alone again after Ellen's death, he had time—too much, it seemed then, as day after day he went to her grave—to think. His development, delayed as he read and pondered during his earlier years as student and teacher, gathered impetus. It first took the form of revolt against what he disliked. What he would have he did not yet know. He knew what he would not have.

One of the forms of worship he most disliked was the sacrament of the Lord's Supper. He did not believe it had been intended to be a permanent institution. He told his congregation he felt he should not remain their minister because he felt he could no longer administer the sacrament, and he wished to do nothing he could not do with his whole heart. He suggested that they omit the bread and wine from Communion.

Having said his say, Emerson went alone to the mountains to think over his position. He had nothing against the Communion ceremony. As far as he was concerned, it could stand to the end of time, but it was not for him. If his congregation agreed to what he had suggested, he would remain. If it did not, he would go. The congregation did not agree. Emerson's resignation was accepted by a vote of thirty of the church's proprietors against twenty-four. Emerson preached his final sermon as minister of the Second Church in the summer of 1832. He had been minister of the Old North for three years.

Fellow ministers were outspoken in their criticism. Some called Emerson's action "Quakerish." Others said it was at least foolish. He had resigned one of the best pastorates in Boston for what they considered a mere whim. Some people whispered loudly that Ralph Waldo Emerson was as mad as Edward had been.

One of those who bitterly disapproved his action was Emerson's redoubtable Aunt Mary, and the wonder is that the tiny but savagely outspoken woman did not tell him so more luridly. Aunt Mary had gloried in her favorite nephew's early success in the ministry. She had heartily approved his marriage. Perhaps it was only the knowledge of the black grief which Ellen's death had caused Emerson that kept her from blazing out.

Aunt Mary had urged Emerson to mend his ways and stay on at the Second Church. She had reminded him of the greatness his ancestors had attained in the Church and of his duty to their memory and to his family. When, despite her insistence, Emerson insisted on going his own way, she virtually cast him off.

Strongly orthodox in her views, Mary Moody Emerson felt that her nephew's objections to administering the Communion were ridiculous. She decided bitterly when it was all over that Emerson had never really loved his holy office, so that it was a good thing he had left it.

Emerson wanted to get away now. His wife was dead. His church was gone. Wonderful beginnings had come to less wonderful ends. He thought of traveling south again. He thought of joining Edward in Porto Rico. Instead, on Christmas Day, 1832, he sailed for Europe in the brig *Jasper*.

The *Jasper* was a small ship of 236 tons which carried mahogany, tobacco, sugar, coffee, cheese, and five passengers who soon were in their staterooms violently seasick. A winter voyage in the North Atlantic is usually rough. The *Jasper*'s quarters were small and dirty. The menu was mostly pork and beans. Emerson held that, at best, the sea was pleasant only where it met the land, yet the harsh voyage began to restore his health and spirits. Dr. Edward Emerson said that his father always throve on physical hardship and took a certain pleasure in it. He did now. Even his sense of humor came back.

The marriage and the career on which he had embarked simultaneously had both collapsed. Figuratively as well as literally, he was at sea. He was perplexed and thoughtful, but not despondent this time. "What under the sun canst thou do then, pale face?" he asked himself flippantly. He answered seriously, "Truly not much, but I can hope."

3

Emerson landed in Malta in early February 1833. It can almost be said that it was at this point that Ralph Waldo Emerson began to be Ralph Waldo Emerson. The actual turning point, if one can be pinpointed, may have been his quitting the Old North Church, but it was with his landing in Europe that the seeking to which his dissatisfactions had brought him began to lead to finding.

Geographically, Emerson had escaped unhappiness and perplexities. He saw for the first time the Old World about which he had read so much that he seemed to have dwelt in it for centuries. More important, he found men. Consciously or unconsciously, he had been searching for kindred minds, for men of intellect and imagination who saw things as he saw them and found the kinds of meanings he found in life. "He was lonely and hungering for friendships with men worthy of the time," his son, Dr. Emerson, wrote.

Emerson awoke in Europe. His doubts about the course of action he had taken vanished. Whereas he had written Aunt Mary from Virginia a few years before that he did not know whether his health had improved one jot during his absence, he wrote her jubilantly soon after landing in Malta that he had left Boston a wasted and peevish invalid but had been mending ever since.

Edward Gibbon opened *The Decline and Fall of the Roman Empire* in 1776 with an account of hearing barefoot friars sing Mass in the temple of Jupiter. Emerson too heard the Christian God worshipped in pagan shrines. He wrote William from Syracuse, Sicily, on February 26 that he had heard Mass sung in an ancient temple of Minerva which was now a Christian cathedral. It was pleasure and wonder that moved Emerson, not the irony Gibbon had felt and expressed.

The churches of Europe awed Emerson with their age and beauty. "How beautiful to have the church always open, so that every tired wayfaring man may come in and be soothed by all that art can suggest of a better world when he is weary with this!" he wrote in his journal. "I hope they will carve and paint and inscribe the walls of our churches in New England before this century . . . is closed. . . . Have the men of America never entered these European churches, that they build such mean edifices at home?"

Emerson had brought letters of introduction with him, but he seldom used them. When he wanted greatly to see a man, he wrote him a letter when he was in his neighborhood, so that the other could judge whether or not he wished to see and know him. If an invitation resulted, Emerson called. He was not a pusher, but he wanted painfully to meet the writers of Europe whom he admired and sometimes reverenced. "Am I who have hung over their works in my chamber not to see these men in the flesh and thank them and interchange some thoughts with them when I am passing their very doors?"

In Florence, Emerson met Horatio Greenough, the American sculptor. Greenough got him an invitation to dinner with Walter Savage Landor, who lived at San

Domenico di Fiesole. The author of *Imaginary Conversations,* known for his petulance and irritability, was decided in his opinions. He would have none of Socrates, whom Emerson had admired since college. He disliked Edmund Burke, whom Emerson liked. He would not admit that he had even heard of some of his caller's favorite contemporary authors. They talked of Byron, of Wordsworth, of George Washington, and of the Elizabethan dramatists. This was such talk as Emerson had never known in Boston or Cambridge. He valued the wit and wisdom of Landor's writing, delighted in Landor's elegant sentences. He came away stimulated anew.

In Rome, Emerson saw the Pope, and heard him bless the palms on Palm Sunday and his choir chant the Passion. He heard the *Miserere* sung in the Sistine Chapel. It sounded to him like the aeolian harp, his favorite music. Everything, he thought, was in good taste. St. Peter's he found beautiful.

From Italy, Emerson went on to Geneva, then to Paris, which he disliked. Though he was happy in meeting and talking with Lafayette, he called Paris "a loud, modern New York of a place."

One dark Sunday morning early in July he landed at the foot of the Tower Stairs in London. He walked up through Cheapside and the Strand to a house in Russell Square, where he took lodgings with a Mrs. Fowler. Emerson was thrilled to feel English soil under his feet for the first time. This was to be the great adventure.

He saw the Duke of Wellington at Westminster Abbey at the funeral of William Wilberforce. He met and talked with John Stuart Mill, the Utilitarian philosopher. On August 5 he went to Highgate and wrote a note asking permission to pay his respects to Samuel Taylor Coleridge.

Coleridge was sixty-one years old. Though it was nearly noon, he was still in bed. His return note said that if Emerson would come at one o'clock, he would see him.

As he describes the poet in *English Traits,* what Emerson saw when he arrived was "a short, thick old man with bright blue eyes and a fine clear complexion, leaning on his cane. He took snuff freely, which presently soiled his cravat and neat black suit."

Almost immediately, Coleridge burst into a diatribe against the foolishness of Unitarianism. He was sorry that Dr. William Ellery Channing, whom he admired, was a Unitarian. He had once been a Unitarian himself and knew what quackery it was. When Emerson admitted that he had been born and bred a Unitarian, Coleridge said, yes, he supposed so, took another breath, and continued his monologue.

When Emerson rose to go, Coleridge asked him whether he liked poetry. Emerson said that he did. Coleridge stood up then and recited lines he had recently composed for his baptismal anniversary.

On August 28, Emerson went to Rydal Mount at Grasmere in the Lake Country of the north of England, to see William Wordsworth. It was to Wordsworth, now sixty-three, that Emerson owed his feeling for nature and his poetic insight into the natural world. Wordsworth's daughters called in their father, who had just returned from a journey. The man who was and is the greatest of the English romantic poets was wearing green goggles to protect his eyes, which at the time were strained and inflamed.

Wordsworth, speaking simply, talked of America. There was vulgarity there, he told Emerson, but it did not matter. That came of the pioneer state of things in the new country. Americans paid too much attention to making money and to politics. American newspapers, he had heard, were atrocious.

Wordsworth took Emerson into his garden where, walking up and down the paths, he had composed so much of his poetry. Then, like Coleridge, he asked whether Emerson would like him to recite some of it. Standing in his garden, his eyes inflamed under the disfiguring goggles, a tooth broken from a fall a few days before, he recited three of his sonnets. The performance was so much like that of a schoolboy declaiming that, despite his worship of the man, Emerson nearly laughed. The poet, Emerson remembered, is always young. Wordsworth struck the same pose while reciting his work that he might have done had he still been seventeen.

When Emerson started to return to his inn, Wordsworth said he would show him a short cut and walked nearly a mile with him, "talking and ever and anon stopping short to impress the word or the verse, and finally parted from me with great kindness and returned across the fields."

After preaching in Edinburgh, Emerson sought out Thomas Carlyle, who was then living at Craigenputtock, a farm in wild and desolate country some sixteen miles from Dumfries. Here Emerson found the man he sought.

The two men were unlike. Carlyle was intolerant, melancholy, misanthropic, where Emerson was gentle and optimistic. Yet they saw themselves in each other. Both were idealists. Both had a passionate love of "the truth." Though Carlyle was eight years older and had already published his essays on German literature, both were at the threshold of their literary careers. "I found the youth I sought in Scotland," Emerson wrote rapturously in his journal, "and good and wise and pleasant he seems to me. . . . I never saw more amiableness than is in his countenance."

They talked like men starved, as perhaps they were. Gaunt and tall, powerful in conversation, Carlyle held forth with great animation to the thirty-year-old stranger from America who looked like an angel. They talked of *Tristram Shandy* and *Robinson Crusoe,* of Edward Gibbon, Socrates, Plato, the magazines, the newspapers. They talked of newer books and writers. Carlyle preferred his pig to many of the writers.

They walked over the long hills, and Emerson talked of the immortality of the soul. Carlyle listened politely while he waited a chance to air more of his strong opinions. London, he told Emerson, was the place and John Stuart Mill had the best brain in London. Goethe was the man to read. Carlyle had learned German ten years before. He talked of English pauperism, of the crowded conditions. Government, he declared, should tell poor men what to do.

This was the beginning of a lifelong friendship and a long trans-Atlantic correspondence between two of the outstanding writers of the nineteenth century, two writers disparate in temperament and manner of expression but alike in their unrelenting search for the values they found.

Soon Emerson went to Liverpool to await ship home. There he spent nine days in the company of Jacob Perkins, inventor of the steam gun, who told him that some day ships powered by steam would cross the Atlantic. While in Liverpool, Emerson took stock of his European journey and its results, and put down the totals in his journal, September 1, 1833.

I thank the Great God who has led me through this European scene . . . He has shown me the men I wished to see,— Landor, Coleridge, Carlyle, Wordsworth; he has thereby comforted and confirmed me in my convictions. Many things I owe to the sight of these men. I shall judge more justly, less timidly, of wise men forevermore. . . .

The comfort of meeting men of genius such as these is that they talk sincerely, they feel themselves to be so rich that they are above the meanness of pretending to knowledge which they have not, and they frankly tell you what puzzles them. But Carlyle—Carlyle is so amiable that I love him.

A month and five days after he set sail, Emerson was back in the United States imbued with a new vitality and a confidence he had never known before. He was glad to be home again, back again to himself. He was still in love with "moral perfection," as he called his dream of the spiritual life. Most important, he would see things from his own viewpoint and not try to see them from the viewpoints of other people. That was the mistake he had made in the ministry.

He went to live with his mother in Newton and almost immediately began to lecture. He spoke as a layman from a platform now, not as a priest from the altar.

Ralph Waldo Emerson had been places and seen things. He had met and talked with great men. He was exhilarated where he had been depressed. He had new thoughts and old thoughts drawn from his sermons to talk about. So, like many a lecturer before and since, he talked about something quite different.

His first lectures were on natural science, about which he knew little or nothing. Again like many lecturers and teachers, he boned up on his subjects, reading enough chemistry, botany, meteorology, and the like for his purposes. Emerson's first lecture subject in Boston was "Water." He followed it with the "Relation of Man to the Globe."

Probably they were not very good lectures, but probably they did their audiences no harm. Certainly, they did Emerson much good. Used to the pulpit, he now got used to the platform, and he liked it. He began a new series of lectures on his travel experiences in Europe. These must have been better and brighter lectures. The ex-minister and ex-teacher developed fast as a popular lecturer at a time when there were few other means of polite diversion that were also entertaining and instructive.

Emerson felt free and alive. As well as lecturing, he was preaching every Sunday at Plymouth, New Bedford, East Lexington, or some other town. The Unitarians in New Bedford offered him their pulpit when Dr. Dewey resigned.

47

Emerson agreed to accept if he did not have to offer prayers at stated intervals in the service. He would pray only when the spirit moved; sometimes he would not pray at all. His terms were not accepted.

A revitalized Emerson who had made up his mind was making other plans for both his career and his personal life. He was determined now to trust to his own instincts. He would rely on himself and his own judgments. "All the mistakes I make arise from forsaking my own station and trying to see the object from another person's point of view," he wrote in his journal. He would not make mistakes from this cause again. Henceforth he would be his own man.

' For a time he thought of moving to the Berkshires in western Massachusetts. The Berkshire mountains and hills were like Wordsworth's Lake Country. Perhaps he could find a place like Carlyle's Craigenputtock which would give him seclusion and inspiration for his writing. He wrote Edward, urging him to come home and join him in a rural retreat in the Berkshires. Edward thanked him and said they would talk it over when, as he planned, he returned to New England the following year.

Emerson wrote William in New York that he hoped to buy a hearth somewhere. In the end, the Berkshires, rural then and rural now, seemed too remote. He needed to be near libraries and lyceums. He depended upon the stimulus of Harvard and intellectual Boston, and Edward would not be coming.

Emerson was in New York when he received word of Edward's death in St. John, Porto Rico. Early privation, searing ambition, and frantic overwork had finished the most promising member of the family. Now Emerson had lost Edward as well as Ellen. In New York, Emerson wrote in his journal, October 1834, "So falls one more pile of hope for this life. I see I am bereft of part of myself." He tried to assuage his grief in poetry. "In Memoriam" is dedicated to Edward Bliss Emerson. In part of that long poem he wrote:

Born for success he seemed,
With grace to win, with heart to hold,
With shining gifts that took all eyes,
With budding power in college-halls,
As pledged in coming days to forge
Weapons to guard the State, or scourge
Tyrants despite their guards or walls.
On his young promise Beauty smiled,
Drew his free homage unbeguiled,
And prosperous Age held out his hand,
And richly his larger future planned,
And troops of friends enjoyed the tide,—
All, all was given, and only health denied.

A month after Edward's death, Emerson and his mother, at the invitation of Dr. Ripley, moved as boarders into the manse in Concord, the ancestral home of the Emersons, where he had spent a year of his boyhood. Charles was already in Concord, where he was studying law under Samuel Hoar and engaged to marry his daughter, Elizabeth. Emerson set about looking for a permanent home for them all.

A point not emphasized by Emerson's biographers, who usually portray him as chiefly dependent on his own exertions in lecturing and writing, is that, economically, Emerson owed his new liberation to his dead young wife. Because of the legacy she had left him, he was free of the necessity of taking the New Bedford or any other church or of finding a regular occupation which would return him an assured income. He could plan on purchase of a home in the place that pleased him best from these funds. Ellen Tucker Emerson's estate also provided him with an income of $1,200 a year. It was not riches, but it was more than a sufficiency. Many large families in the

1830s, and for almost a century afterward, lived on less.

This inheritance gave Emerson the freedom to read and write and lecture as he pleased. He could walk as he willed and talk from the platform for little or nothing if the audience was one he wished to talk to and he had something he wished to say. Practically, Ellen Tucker bequeathed Emerson his freedom.

He was determined now "not to utter any speech, poem or book that is not entirely and peculiarly my work. I will say at public lectures and the like, those things which I have meditated for their own sake, and not for the first time with a view to that occasion."

In 1835 he wrote and read in Boston lectures on Michelangelo, Martin Luther, John Milton, George Fox, and Edmund Burke. He prefaced these lectures before appreciative audiences with an introductory lecture on the tests of great men. They found meaning and purpose by looking within themselves. They had humor. Shakespeare, Luther, and Lafayette worked in broad daylight with red cheeks.

Emerson followed his biographical series with another series of ten lectures on English literature. He had found his lifework, and he reveled in it. Though he complained often in later years of the wearisome travel and the hardships of the lecture circuit, he needed to talk and to be heard. He needed to use his gift, an actor's gift really, of tone, timing, subtle emphasis. He needed the response of an appreciative audience, and his audiences, growing and more enthusiastic each year, needed Emerson and adored him. He spoke as he had preached, simply and sincerely. His voice was delightful. He could give even carefully memorized material the effect of spontaneity. He seemed simply to be sharing his rich mind and imagination with his hearers, and his hearers, from the simplest to the most complex, were flattered and thrilled.

Most of his lecture material came from his journal. He called it his savings bank. On January 1, 1834, he wrote in it, "I grow richer because I have somewhere to deposit my earnings; and fractions are worth more to me because corresponding fractions are waiting here that shall be made integers by their addition."

Gone was the depression and listlessness brought on by the feeling of failure. Emerson was eagerly busy. He was writing and giving his lectures, corresponding with Coleridge and Carlyle, preaching on Sundays, writing his first book.

He was happy. By virtue of birth and family, he knew everyone of importance in Concord. He was walking and writing; the two always went together for him. He had the solitude he needed and, seventeen miles away, a market for his wares and the incentive to produce more.

In Concord, he wrote, the northwest winds and the snows kept him guarded all winter. The hills and sandbanks between him and the city protected him in summer. The Concord River flowed placidly past the Old Manse. The pine woods were near by. The wooded shores of blue Walden Pond invited. Emerson sought them to think and await inspiration. The pine woods were his real study, he said; his study at home was only his library and writing room. "All my thoughts are foresters. I have scarce a daydream on which the breath of the pines has not blown and their shadows waved."

He and his mother left Dr. Ripley's manse and rented a house, but he asked William in a letter whether a year hence they should not build a house on their grandfather's hill facing the hills of Wachusett, Monadnoc, and the setting sun. Instead, he purchased the house he had rented. It was the old Coolidge place, a square frame house on the edge of the village toward Lincoln and Lexington which at first Emerson called a mean place. It was not. The seller told him that it had cost him $7,800. Emerson paid him $3,500 for the house and a little more than two acres of land surrounding it. He planned to spend another four or five hundred dollars enlarging it to provide quarters for Charles and his affianced bride.

Emerson himself planned to remarry. In Plymouth he had met Lydia Jackson. Their home would be in Concord and in this house. He made that clear in a letter to his fiancée, a letter which also made clear to her what he had come to realize about himself. Emerson knew now what he was and how he had to live.

"I must win you to love it [Concord]," he wrote. "I am born a poet. That is my nature and vocation. My singing, be sure, is very husky, and is for the most part in prose. Still am I a poet in the sense of a perceiver and dear lover of the harmonies that are in the soul and in matter, and especially of the correspondence between these and those. A sunset, a forest, a snow-storm, a certain river-view, are more to me than many friends, and do ordinarily divide my day with books. Wherever I go, therefore, I guard and study my rambling propensities with a care that is ridiculous to people, but to me is the care of my high calling." Other towns, he said, might provide these things as well, but they were not Concord. Concord he loved.

When the town was two hundred years old, Emerson was asked to give the bicentennial address. He read and studied Concord history. He talked to survivors of the battle at Concord Bridge. He garnered details from the diary of his Continental Army chaplain grandfather. Men who had fought at Concord were on the platform with him when he spoke on Saturday, September 12, 1835. It was for the dedication of the battle monument on Patriot's Day, April 19, 1836, that he wrote the "Concord Hymn."

By the rude bridge that arched the flood,
    Their flag to April's breeze unfurled,
Here once the embattled farmers stood
    And fired the shot heard round the world.

The foe long since in silence slept;
   Alike the conqueror silent sleeps;
And Time the ruined bridge has swept
   Down the dark stream which seaward creeps.

On this green bank, by this soft stream,
   We set to-day a votive stone;
That memory may their deed redeem,
   When, like our sires, our sons are gone.

Spirit, that made these heroes dare
   To die, and leave their children free,
Bid Time and Nature gently spare
   The shaft we raise to them and thee.

The day after his bicentennial address, Sunday, Emerson spent with his family in the Old Manse. The next day, Monday, September 14, 1835, he went to Plymouth and was married to Lydia Jackson. Liking the sound of it better, he changed her given name as well as her surname and brought Lidian Jackson Emerson home to Concord.

Emerson's love of Concord and his patriotism were not merely sentimental. Many of the dreamers and reformers with whom he was soon to be associated kept aloof from local or national affairs. A number of them, like Henry David Thoreau, even refused to vote. They looked on government as an alien and inimical force. Emerson saw it as an activity in which he shared.

He had the educated man's contempt for the self-seeking of most politicians and he despised the machinations of party politics, but he considered it his privilege as well as his duty not only to vote but also, insofar as he was able, to participate in Concord affairs.

Though he never spoke at them, he attended town meetings regularly and approved the common sense of many of his sturdy neighbors. He joined the Concord Fire Association, and the leather bucket and green baize bag always hung over the entry on the back stairs of his home, though, as the town soon had an engine and a regular fire department, they were not used. He served on the Concord school board for many years. He was on the board of the library and of the Athenaeum. He even became a town office holder soon after he was married.

With all the enthusiasm of the new householder, Emerson was at work in his garden one day—he was never much good at it—when a man came and told him that a pig was loose and damaging a neighbor's property. It was so Emerson learned that, in accordance with the town's demure custom of bestowing the honor on a newly married man, he had been appointed one of Concord's pig catchers.

Whether he went and duly routed the pig is not reported. At any rate, though he continued to prune his trees, he soon gave up gardening, turning the work over to Henry Thoreau and other willing friends. He complained that whether he planted radishes or oak trees everything came up tulips, Lidian's favorite flower, and so he went back to his reading, writing, and walking. He had other gardens to cultivate and other fruit to produce.

The book which he had written while still living in the Old Manse was published in 1836. A small book of less than one hundred pages, unsigned but quickly attributed to him, *Nature* was Emerson's first open letter to the world. In *Nature* he stated his beliefs and drew his dreams. In language that soared and sang, then rang with certainty, he told of the identity of God and man through nature and pictured the ideal world visible less through thought than through intuitive understanding and poetic insight.

4

Nature was hard to understand in 1836. It is difficult to read now. It could not be read then and it cannot be read now as simple and logical argument. Emerson's mind did not work that way, and he did not write that way. *Nature,* though it is charged with provocative thought, is more poetry than the prose which, in form, it is.

Emerson could not begin with A and progress methodically through B, C, and D to a firm conclusion at Z. He saw in sudden flashes of insight and wrote what he saw in his journal. He understood mysteries in sudden bursts of inspiration or in longer moods of quiet communion with the thoughts of Plato, Shakespeare, Montaigne, and other writers as these were shot through with the winds over the fields of Concord or made fragrant with the scent of the pines. He became convinced of truths in moments of intense conviction, perhaps as he was taking a stroll about Walden Pond on a sunny afternoon or walking under the stars at night. He put these convictions into his journal too.

A phrase, even a word, perhaps a whole sentence that seemed to illumine came to him. He put it down for later use. Emerson could achieve a radiant lucidity in a sentence.

He could not maintain it for a paragraph. His chapters are apt to confound because they are confused.

When he wanted to compose a lecture, an essay, or a book, he mined his journal like a prospector, not methodically like a mining engineer. He might find a pearl at F, a sapphire at J, an opalescent glow at M, jade at Q, and a veritable diamond or ruby at V. These he jumbled together in a handful of gems that flashed with fire, gleamed with multicolored reflections, and often dazzled with a variegated brilliance. Emerson dazzled or he induced a delighted surrender, akin to his own in creating; he intoxicated with splendor in color and the music of his words, rather than convinced.

There is much plain common sense in Emerson. He could and did say simple things in a simple but striking way. There is much that is more complicated, for he thought and wrote of the complexities and perplexities of existence that the best minds have thought about since the beginning of time. There is also much that is mystical, for, like most religious and spiritual thinkers, he was a mystic—one who reaches over and past verifiable, factual, sense-available evidence to understand through direct insight or intuition. Because of the nature of his subjects, God, man, truth, the soul, Emerson could often state profound truths of which he felt certain only through comparison or word-painting.

These parts of Emerson's writing you understand much as you "understand" a symphony or a sunset. You understand Emerson, as he understood life and the world of thought and spirit, through your feelings and your imagination, through your response to the magic of his words.

When he sent Carlyle a copy of *Nature*, Emerson described the book as an opening wedge to later writing that might prove more worthy and significant. He meant it, really, to be more than that. As the first book of an original writer often does, *Nature* stated the position he had reached at this time, the things he thought worth thinking and writing about, and all that he could yet say about these things in as explicit a way as he could say it.

Emerson's subject in his first small book was very large. It was man and his world, or, in Emerson's words, nature and the soul. These make up the universe of which man is aware. He is aware of his inner self and he is aware of the natural world which surrounds him. Emerson wanted men to be aware not only of the appearances of the world of nature but of its inner being too.

He began *Nature* by pleading that men look at it and see it as it is, not as it has been reported by the older writers. Then he went on to consider his subject in different ways.

It is dangerous and unfair to try to translate all that Emerson said in *Nature* into overly simple terms. If what Emerson had to say in the book could have been stated in a sentence or two or put down and solved like a simple problem in arithmetic, Emerson would have said it that way. It could not and he did not. In a way, he was saying what the Bible says in a sentence he considered contains the first and last lesson of religion: "The things which are seen are temporal; but the things which are not seen are eternal."

Emerson believed and said that the visible world of nature, which we can see, is only the outward sign and symbol of the spiritual life which underlies nature, a spiritual life which we cannot see. A landscape, a sunset, a tree is but the reflection of the thought of God. Just as words are merely symbols for facts, these facts of nature— landscape, tree, sunset, and all else—are but symbols of spiritual facts. He believed and wrote in *Nature* that truth and beauty and goodness are but different aspects of the all which is God.

57

Every natural fact is a symbol of some spiritual fact. Every appearance in nature corresponds to some state of the mind, and that state of the mind can only be described by presenting that natural appearance as its picture. An enraged man is a lion, a cunning man is a fox, a firm man is a rock, a learned man is a torch. A lamb is innocence; a snake is subtle spite; flowers express to us the delicate affections. Light and darkness are our familiar expressions for knowledge and ignorance; and heat for love. Visible distance, behind and before us, is respectively our image of memory and hope.

Nature serves man, Emerson said, in useful ways. It provides him with foods and minerals, with a climate in which he can live, with materials for his home, but it gives him more. "A nobler want of man is served by nature, namely the love of beauty." The human eye instinctively seeks beauty and finds it in the face of the earth and sky.

Emerson said that he loved nature as a child loves it. "I expand and live in the warm days like corn and melons." He loved it too, and more deeply, as a poet loves it. He sought in nature the truth which is also beauty. He did not expect to find it through reason but through intuition, through direct knowledge and awareness. Science, Emerson said in the final section of *Nature,* has only half-sight.

Always, Emerson believed less in what you can see and prove than in what you can feel and know. He thought that the best moments in life are those in which you are sure and are convinced that something you feel—like the beauty in a sunrise or a sense of truth and utter happiness in the quiet of a church or in the stillness of the woods—is true and good. He found reality of this kind in poetry and religion.

A tall red oak is different from a woodchuck or a mountain or a granite boulder. There are all kinds of different things in nature. There are lakes, pine trees, robins, and a thousand other forms of life. They are all different. They are all different, but something in them is the same. There is a oneness, a unity, in nature which makes all things, different from each other as they may be, a part of the same whole. Emerson felt this oneness in all things.

Every man is different from every other man, but together all of them are man. Emerson thought that in some mysterious way even God and man are the same. "God in us worships God," he once wrote. In other words, he thought that there is some essential element in God and in man that is the same. It is through what is like God in him that man recognizes and worships God.

Most of what we know, we know through our five senses. We find out things through seeing, hearing, tasting, smelling, and feeling. We see that the leaves of trees are green. We hear that the noise of thunder is loud. We taste the sweetness of honey or the bitterness of a nut. We feel the coldness of ice and the heat of fire. We know other things, though, which we cannot learn through our senses. Our knowledge of truth, of justice, of freedom, is knowledge of this other kind, which we call abstract. In the *Critique of Pure Reason,* published in 1781, a German thinker, Immanuel Kant, called such knowledge "transcendental," because it transcends or goes over and beyond ordinary reason.

Emerson believed that by the very nature of their being, men possess such transcendental knowledge. In time "Transcendentalism" came to mean more than Immanuel Kant had intended. English poets, then writers and speakers in New England, added more mystic and misty ideas to it. Emerson, who disliked the word and did not consider himself a Transcendentalist, came to be looked upon as the head of the Transcendental movement—which itself was looked upon almost as a new religion in New England in the 1840s and 1850s.

Whatever else Emerson said or intimated in *Nature,* his first book brought him to the world's notice as an original thinker and writer of poetic force. Comparatively few copies were sold. *Nature* was unintelligible to many who tried to read it, but it impressed those who could read and follow his thought. At least they realized that here was a new and bold concept stated in vivid and provocative words.

Carlyle was delighted. He wrote Emerson that the little azure-colored book gave him true satisfaction. "I read it, then lent it to all my acquaintances that had a sense for such things; from whom a similar verdict always came back." Prophetically, Carlyle called *Nature* a foundation or ground plan on which Emerson could build "whatever of great and true has been given you to build."

Undoubtedly it was *Nature* and Emerson's growing reputation as a speaker which led to the invitation to deliver the Phi Beta Kappa oration at Harvard the next year. This was a signal honor for the young man who only a few years before had offended many in Cambridge by leaving his pulpit in Boston's Second Church.

Emerson had moved to Concord in part to be near his brother Charles. Oliver Wendell Holmes called Charles Chauncey Emerson "the most angelic adolescent my eyes ever beheld." Charles was gifted and proud. The young lawyer had imbibed many of his moral and intellectual ideas from Ralph Waldo Emerson, who was about seven years older than he. In turn, his character and conversation inspired and stimulated Emerson.

In a letter to Carlyle, October 7, 1835, Emerson called Charles his other presence. Mentally and emotionally the brothers were very close. They were friends and companions as well as brothers. They were of a kind. As Emerson wrote Carlyle in a later letter, "I have put so much dependence on his gifts, that we made but one man together; for I needed never to do what he could do by noble nature, much better than I."

In 1836 Emerson was adding apartments to his house for Charles and Elizabeth Hoar when Charles Emerson was stricken as Edward had been. Immediately, Emerson started south with him to seek a milder climate. They stopped in New York, and the sick man went for a carriage drive with their mother, promising Emerson they would continue their journey south the next day. When mother and son returned from their ride, Charles walked unaided into the house, sat down on the stairs, fainted, and never recovered. He died May 9, 1836.

"Beautiful without any parallel in my experience of young men, was his life, happiest his death," Emerson wrote in his journal. "Clean and sweet was his life, untempted almost, and his actions on others all-healing, uplifting and fragrant. . . . His senses were those of a Greek. I owe to them a thousand observations. To live with him was like living with a great painter. I used to say that I had no leave to see things till he had pointed them out, and afterwards I never ceased to see them."

The fellowship of the four brothers was finished. William was far away. The other two were dead. Emerson stood alone now, and it is possible that he never ceased to feel a certain loneliness. Their boyhood struggles and the shared intensity of their desire to attain eminence had held the brothers close together.

Ellen, Edward, and Charles were gone. Emerson grieved again, but he had other resources now. His need to satisfy himself as well as the expectations of his Aunt Mary had not been stilled, but it had begun to be appeased.

He was a man of modest independent means, firmly established in his own home. His first son, Waldo, was born in October 1836, and he delighted in the child. Emerson had been the pastor of a leading Boston church and, had he so chosen, could still have occupied its pulpit. He had met and talked on terms of equality with Wordsworth, Coleridge, and Carlyle. He had won applause and growing fame as a lecturer. His first book had brought him the respectful attention of those whose opinions he valued. He

61

had suffered loss and grief not once but three times, and each time faced it down. He was to suffer comparable loss once more and suffer even more deeply, but he could not know that yet.

Zeal tempered by suffering, Emerson could be as serene inwardly as he always appeared in public and even with his intimates. That serenity, born of inner sureness, had always, perhaps, been an element more basic in his temperament than the ambition whipped on by Aunt Mary and whetted by competition with his brothers.

Emerson was emerging. He had begun to make his mark. Now at Harvard, where it mattered most in intellectual New England and mattered most to him, he would burn the mark in deeper. He had, he knew always, been born for victory. The 1837 Phi Beta Kappa oration could be his first important triumph, and it was.

Emerson delivered his address August 31, 1837, before the Harvard chapter of the honorary scholarship society which had been founded at the College of William and Mary in Virginia the same year the United States declared its independence. He titled it "The American Scholar."

James Russell Lowell called it "an event without any former parallel in our literary annals, a scene to be always treasured in the memory for its picturesqueness and its inspiration." Oliver Wendell Holmes, exclaiming that nothing like it had been heard in the halls of Harvard since Samuel Adams debated there, said, "This grand oration was our intellectual Declaration of Independence. . . . No listener ever forgot that address, and among all the noble utterances of the speaker it may be questioned if one ever contained more truth in language more like that of immediate inspiration." Young men were inspired. They listened and heeded as if a prophet had spoken. Some, like Henry David Thoreau, who graduated that year, were deeply and permanently influenced.

Tall, thin, with narrow sloping shoulders, a small head

but a high forehead, Emerson spoke as quietly as always. Idealism shone in his face and sounded in the lyric grace of his words. He spoke simply, using homely illustrations, then words and sentences of soaring splendor, then homely illustrations again. Seeming to think of them as he went along, he repeated many of the ideas he had first proposed in *Nature,* but his ordering was different, and there was the effect of magical simplicity in his utterance. He was preaching, as Emerson always preached when he spoke, and he converted through a wonderful contagion.

What Emerson said was, Know yourself—trust yourself—be yourself.

He began with a stirring plea for an independent American culture, a distinctive American approach to thought and expression, particularly in poetry. It was an idea that was in the air at the time, a popular idea, but Emerson's statement of it was stirring as no previous plea had been.

Perhaps, he said, the time had already come, "when the sluggard intellect of this continent will look from under its iron lids and fill the postponed expectation of the world with something better than the exertions of mechanical skill. Our day of dependence, our long apprenticeship to the learning of other lands, draws to a close. The millions that around us are rushing into life, cannot always be fed on the sere remains of foreign harvests. Events, actions arise, that must be sung, that will sing themselves."

Characteristically, Emerson spoke in provocative generalities. He did not say specifically what he meant. He did not try to translate his plea into concrete terms and say exactly what should be written in America that should be different in thought and language from what was thought and written elsewhere. Emerson's mission always was to inspire, not to lay out blueprints.

Having made his plea, Emerson went on rapidly to what he really had to say. He defined the scholar. He listed the elements of the scholar's education in what he saw as the order of their importance, then outlined the duties of the scholar. He did this with the straight-line approach that Emerson at his best could achieve. As he so often did, he cut through peripheral complexities to the central meaning and said clearly what other men might fumble to phrase. Once he had said it, they knew it for what they had meant all along.

The scholar, Emerson told his enraptured audience, is "Man Thinking." The first and most important influence on the scholar and his thinking is nature.

> Every day, the sun; and, after sunset, Night and her stars. Ever the winds blow; ever the grass grows. Every day, men and women, conversing—beholding and beholden. The scholar is he of all men whom this spectacle most engages. . . . There is never a beginning, there is never an end, to the inexplicable continuity of this web of God, but always circular power returning into itself.

It would be hard for anyone else to say this better than Emerson said it, and no one ever has. The scholar sees, Emerson said, that nature is the counterpart of his soul, matching it part for part. "One is seal and one is print. Its beauty is the beauty of his own mind. Its laws are the laws of his own mind."

This is the Emersonian mysticism again: the identity of man and nature, the identity of man and God. This is an awareness which some men feel and know as Emerson knew and felt it and as he felt men should know such unanalyzable truths: by intuition, by immediate perception. Few men have stated the idea of man's oneness with his universe better.

The next influence on the mind of the scholar is books. Emerson called them "the mind of the past," for it is through books that the past comes to us. He did not minimize books and their importance, but he warned against too great a dependence upon books. This was strange doctrine at Harvard, but as soon as he said it, its truth became evident to many of his young listeners. Read, Emerson told them, but do not make reading the end of study. If you would be a scholar, if you would be Man Thinking, you must think for yourself and trust your own thoughts. "Meek young men grow up in libraries, believing it their duty to accept the views which Cicero, which Locke, which Bacon, have given; forgetful that Cicero, Locke, and Bacon were only young men in libraries when they wrote these books. . . . Books are for the scholar's idle times. When he can read God directly, the hour is too precious to be wasted in other men's transcriptions of their readings."

Action comes after nature and books in influencing the mind of the scholar. It was a mistaken notion, Emerson said, that the scholar should be a recluse. The true scholar dwells in no ivory tower. He mingles in the world of men and women, observing, and not only observing but participating. The true scholar lives an active life. There is still, he said, virtue in the hoe and the spade for learned as well as unlearned hands.

All of the duties of Man Thinking, Emerson summed up in the one phrase that recurs again and again as central in his thought and writing—Trust yourself. In "The American Scholar," he shortened the adjuration to one hyphenated word, "self-trust."

The scholar must trust his own highest self. He must blaze his own course. He must be true to his instinct to seek out and know the truth. "He is the world's eye. He is the world's heart." He must see clearly, feel his heart beat in unison with his universe of nature, the past, and life about him. He will not be taken in or deluded by appearance. He will be free and brave, and he will not mistake the temporary fad or fancy for eternal truth.

The scholar must trust himself, his knowledge, and his judgment. "Let him not quit his belief that a popgun is a popgun, though the ancient and honorable of the earth affirm it to be the crack of doom."

By knowing himself, by searching his own mind and thoughts, the scholar will come on truths that are universal, that are true for all men as well as for him. By discovering the secrets of his own mind, he will discover the secrets of all minds. The true scholar is no poor-eyed clerk poring over books and manuscripts. He is no pedant. Summarizing near the end of his Phi Beta Kappa oration, Emerson defined him again:

> The scholar is that man who must take up into himself all the ability of the time, all the contributions of the past, all the hopes of the future. . . . If there be one lesson more than another which should pierce his ear, it is, The world is nothing, the man is all; in yourself is the law of all nature . . .

America was not keeping its promises, Emerson said at the end of his address. The mind of the young country was being taught to aim at low material ends. Only the complacent and the decorous prospered. "Young men of the fairest promise, who begin life upon our shores, inflated by the mountain winds, shined upon by all the stars of God" turned in disgust from the conduct of business or turned drudges or simply died. (Was Emerson thinking of Edward?) Young men had to see "that if the single man plant himself indomitably on his instincts, and there abide, the huge world will come round to him."

This was the lesson which Henry Thoreau and others like him took away from Emerson's Phi Beta Kappa oration: Know themselves, trust themselves, be themselves. They left exhilarated and determined by the words Emerson spoke in his conclusion: "We will walk on our own feet; we will work with our own hands; we will speak our own minds."

Not quite a year later, July 15, 1838, Emerson spoke again at Harvard, this time before the graduating class of the Harvard Divinity School. This time the results were far different.

Obeying the precepts he had laid down in "The American Scholar," Emerson trusted himself. He said what he meant and had to say. He also trusted his listeners to understand and share his opinions, characteristically assuming them to have an intelligence equal in kind and scope to his own. His trust was misplaced, or Emerson was tactless in using this platform and this occasion to say what he did. If "The American Scholar" was a triumph, "The Divinity School Address," speaking in practical terms, was a disaster.

"The Divinity School Address" rings with even greater conviction and burns with even greater intensity than "The American Scholar." Emerson must have written it with rapt concentration and delivered it with courage and hope. In a way it was an apologia. In describing his interpretation of Christian religious thought and urging it on the young ministers who were just quitting the classroom for the pulpit, he was describing the attitudes and the practice which had led him to abandon his Boston pulpit. Besides being his apologia, "The Divinity School Address" was his plan for the redemption of the Church, which he saw as failing in its mission and in its hold on the people.

Emerson, as he had told Lidian, was born a poet. He was not born a theologian. He could not abide forms and systems. He found them barren and meaningless. He *knew* that truth and beauty and love and light and God and life were one and that they matched the highest instincts and impulses of man, and he spoke from that knowledge about that knowledge. That to him was true religion, and all the trappings were false.

A speaker in this place on this occasion might have been expected to congratulate the hopeful young ministers on their choice of profession, congratulate them again on having successfully completed an arduous course of study, and urge them to go out and apply all they had learned. Most such speakers did and most still do.

Instead, Emerson told his listeners that much they had been learning in divinity school was useless, that some of it was wrong, and that most of the conventional ways of preaching and worship were bad. He urged them, practically, to forget much of what they had been taught and to preach and lead their congregations in a different fashion.

The opening of his "Divinity School Address" was lyric and happy, a poem in itself: "In this refulgent summer, it has been a luxury to draw the breath of life. The grass grows, the buds burst, the meadow is spotted with fire and gold in the tint of flowers. The air is full of birds, and sweet with the breath of the pine, the balm-of-Gilead, and the new hay."

There was an equal beauty apparent to men when their hearts were open to the sentiment of virtue. "When in innocency or when by intellectual perception he attains to say,—'I love the right; Truth is beautiful within and without for evermore. Virtue, I am thine; save me; use me; thee will I serve, day and night, in great, in small . . . — then is the end of creation answered, and God is well pleased."

He would not attempt to explain what is unexplainable. ". . . love, fear, justice, appetite, man, and God, interact. These laws refuse to be adequately stated. They will not be written out on paper, or spoken by the tongue." Such things, he said, could be known only by intuition and insight. To Emerson, religious sentiment and poetry were the same, and so he spoke of them. Virtue is light and life. Evil is death. Man *knows* this. Thus, "the fountain of all good" is in man himself.

Having established his position once again, Emerson went on to point out what he called the two errors in the teaching of Christianity. The first error was that Christ was treated like an Oriental demigod instead of as a man who knew and realized the potentialities of man and had direct knowledge of man's soul. "He saw with open eye the mystery of the soul. Drawn by its severe harmony, ravished with its beauty, he lived in it, and had his being there. Alone in all history he estimated the greatness of man. One man was true to what is in you and me. He saw that God incarnates himself in man, and evermore goes forth anew to take possession of his World. He said, . . . 'I am divine. Through me, God acts; through me, speaks. Would you see God, see me; or see thee, when thou also thinkest as I now think.' "

This was a long way from the Puritan doctrine of man born in sin and evil. It was a long way in 1838 even from the comparative liberalism of the Unitarian Church. That church, said Emerson, like other Christian groups, dwelt with undue exaggeration on the person of Jesus as a super-natural being. By obeying their own highest selves, as Christ did, all men share in his divinity.

The second error in contemporary preaching, Emerson said, was in teaching that revelations were of the past. This made a dead form of a continuing and ever-present revelation of the beauty of virtue to all men.

Ministers preached of the past and its miracles. The real miracle is now and for everyone. Instead of being told that man is an infinite soul with all the earth and heavens passing in his mind, "that he is drinking forever the soul of God," men are cheated and depressed in their churches by a dead and deadening formalism.

He had once heard a preacher, Emerson said, who had sorely tempted him to say that he would go to church no more. There was no life, no reality in what he preached. Outside it was snowing. Emerson watched the snow through a window as the minister droned on. "The snow-storm was real, the preacher merely spectral. . . . He had no

"Would you see God . . ."

one word intimating that he had ever laughed or wept, was married or in love, had been commended, or cheated, or chagrined. If he had ever lived and acted, we were none the wiser for it." This minister did not convert life into truth, which was his job. Such men taught nothing of real value. The result, Emerson said, was that he had heard "a devout person, who prized the Sabbath, say in bitterness of heart, 'On Sundays, it seems wicked to go to church.' "

(On December 3, 1837, he had written in his journal, "Lidian says, it is wicked to go to church Sundays." A few days later he noted that his son Waldo could walk unaided. This item of real life seemed to him more important than much that he heard in church. God walked in Waldo, as in him, as in all men. At church Emerson heard much preaching of the greatness of Christ. Christ had preached the greatness of men. That was what he was trying so earnestly to tell his hearers now. Once when someone asked him whether he preferred two sermons or one on Sundays, Emerson said one. If it was good, it gave him something to think about; if it was bad, one was enough. Often Emerson was disheartened when he heard what he called false preaching in church. Sometimes he was amused. This same summer he noted in his journal, "Dr. Ripley prays for rain with great explicitness on Sunday, and on Monday the showers fell. When I spoke of the speed with which his prayers were answered, the good man looked modest.")

Not worship through dead forms, not glorification of the past, not deification of the person of Christ and talk of bygone miracles, but direct visions of the truth of present life, recognition of the miracle of man's immediate relationship to nature and God, awareness of the divine in man that Christ himself had preached—these were what Emerson admonished his young listeners to go forth and give their people.

There must have been young men, newly graduated and licensed to preach, who listened intently to Ralph Waldo Emerson that day and left his presence changed men. There were liberal religious thinkers like the eminent William Ellery Channing and Theodore Parker, men who distrusted set dogmas, who approved. Others, the established leaders of Unitarianism, listened with set lips and condemned bitterly what they heard as apostasy and heresy. It was radicalism and worse from one who was himself a graduate of the Harvard Divinity School and had been licensed to preach by a board of Unitarian ministers.

Offended and frightened, they attacked quickly and with intent to annihilate. Official Harvard was horrified. Andrews Norton, who had been professor of Sacred Literature in the Divinity School and represented the entrenched conservative element of Unitarianism, strove to demolish Emerson, first in the *Boston Daily Advertiser,* then in an address, delivered the next year, "The Latest Form of Infidelity." *The Christian Examiner* disavowed and disowned Emerson's stand. Emerson was attacked in speech, in sermons, and in print.

Even his friend the Reverend Henry Ware, who had preceded him at the Second Church, disapproved. He wrote Emerson that some of his opinions might only undermine the influence and authority of Christianity. He sent Emerson a sermon he had preached in which he suggested more conventional additions to the opinions Emerson had stated.

Emerson, though he had known in advance that he might shock some of his older hearers, was aghast at the reaction he had provoked. He would not speak out in his own defense. He kept silent and avoided participation in the controversy he had aroused. He was not a controversialist. He had no skill in debate, and he knew it. In part of a longer letter that he wrote to Henry Ware he said, with marked self-knowledge:

72

I could not give an account of myself if challenged. I could not possibly give you one of the arguments you covertly hint at, on which any doctrine of mine stands; for I do not know what arguments are in reference to any expression of a thought. I delight in telling what I think, but if you ask me how I dare say so, or why it is so, I am the most helpless of mortal men. I do not even see that either of these questions admits of an answer. So that in the present droll position of my affairs, when I see myself suddenly raised to the importance of a heretic, I am very uneasy when I revert to the supposed duties of such a personage, who is to make good his thesis against all comers. I certainly shall do no such thing. I shall read what you and other good men write, as I have always done, glad when you speak my thoughts, and skipping the page that has nothing for me.

When he graduated from Harvard, Emerson had hoped to become a professor of rhetoric, a teacher of speech and prose writing. If he had ever hoped—and he had—that Harvard would offer him such a post, he could forget it. Though he had demonstrated his exceptional abilities, Harvard wanted no more of him now.

In *Nature,* in "The American Scholar," and in "The Divinity School Address" Emerson had asserted and made good his right to be heard. Though she had not foreseen that her nephew might be heralded as a heretic, Aunt Mary Moody Emerson could not complain that he remained unknown, but she found much else to complain of, and complained loudly.

Emerson and his Aunt Mary had become partially reconciled after his defection from the ministry. Emerson's devotion to his aunt never wavered, but hers to him fluctuated with her uncertain moods and with the changes in his domestic life and his career. Also, it was not as easy for Lidian and the more polite world to accept the rude speech and sometimes crude behavior of the aunt who had done so much for Emerson and meant so much to him when he was a boy.

After a row at the dinner table in the Emerson home in Concord, Aunt Mary announced that she would never enter her nephew's house again unless brought there in a litter. Then she decided she would not come even if she were carried in. After this, when she was in Concord she boarded elsewhere and, as everywhere she went in her ceaseless wanderings, in the cheapest place she could find. Once when she refused to pay more than three dollars a week, Emerson and Elizabeth Hoar quietly paid that additional two dollars a week justifiably asked by her landlord.

As Aunt Mary grew older she grew more fantastic, and she could be vindictive. She did not suffer fools gladly. When someone's conversation began to annoy her, she would ask abruptly how the speaker's cat was or order the other out of eye and earshot. Sometimes she sent people on trumped-up errands.

Aunt Mary made it very clear that she had no use for any of the Transcendentalists or what she saw as their nonsense. Like most people, she tolerated only her own kind of nonsense. She was outraged now and scandalized by "The Divinity School Address." Self-taught out of the older religious books she had devoured as a girl and still implicitly believed, she would have none of this newfangled ungodliness and sided with the ministers who attacked the address and its author. If she was pleased and proud of the stature Emerson was achieving in thought and letters, she certainly was not going to let him see it.

5

In Concord, Emerson became a member of two clubs. He was invited to join the Social Circle in 1839 and gladly accepted. This group was composed of twenty-five of Concord's leading citizens. There were doctors, lawyers, farmers, merchants, millers, and mechanics in the club, which met at the homes of its various members, sometimes at Emerson's, on Tuesday nights.

Emerson delighted in the group. He called it much the best society he had ever known. The Social Circle, he said, was made up of "the solidest of men who yield the solidest of gossip." Emerson liked gossip and was always frank to admit it. He liked the talk of practical men about practical things. He valued people who could do things, whether it was write a good book, plow a straight furrow, or lay a brick wall that would stand up. Emerson did not like to be away from home Tuesday evenings in the winter months lest he miss a meeting of the Social Circle.

The Circle was part of his everyday Concord life. Membership in it meant that he belonged, that he had been accepted by the proud little community which his ancestor, the Reverend Peter Bulkeley, had founded.

For privacy, and to extend his gardens and orchard, Emerson added to the original two acres he had acquired with his house until he had a small farm of nine acres. There was always a horse and one or two cows. Emerson loved the place. "When I bought my farm," he wrote in his journal, "I did not know what a bargain I had in the bluebirds, bobolinks, and thrushes which were not charged in the bill. As little did I guess what sublime mornings and sunsets I was buying, what reaches of landscape, and what fields and lanes for a tramp." A young schoolteacher, John Thoreau, Henry's cheerful and more sociable brother, nailed a bluebird box on the Emerson barn, and every year for fifteen years there were bluebirds in it.

Though, through lack of manual skill and because it took more time than he could afford, he was forced to relinquish his gardening to friends and later, as his domain expanded, to keep a hired man, Emerson would go into his fields to help with the hay if a storm threatened. He liked to prune his own fruit trees and pick his own apples and pears: Gravensteins, Flemish Beauties, Pumpkin-Sweetings, and Seckels. He was proud of his gardens and always sent exhibits to the Cattle Show. He admired farmers and their work with the land and spoke often before agricultural societies. Ephraim Bull, the horticulturist who developed the fragrant and juicy, bluish-black Concord grape, was a neighbor he enjoyed.

A less pleasant neighbor, the only one in Concord to make himself deliberately obnoxious, moved a shack to a lot where it was an eyesore from the Emerson house. The Social Circle saw and disapproved. One night a number of Concord's young men borrowed baize firemen's jackets from Mr. Rice's store, got hooks, ropes, and ladders, and marched silently to the spot. They pulled the old frame building down with a crash and vanished into the night, which echoed to the roars of the building's enraged owner.

Besides adding to his little farm, Emerson bought more

land outside the village in order to preserve and protect a spot he loved. He purchased eleven acres of land on the shore of Walden Pond for $8.10 an acre. When it was pointed out to him that these might be spoiled if the wrong man got hold of adjacent land, he bought another three or four acres for an additional $125. He wrote William, "I am now land-lord and water-lord of fourteen acres, more or less, on the shores of Walden, and can raise my own blackberries." Emerson loved to work in his Walden wood-lot with hatchet and pruning shears. He could spend the whole day happily busy there. He said he thought the birds and trees knew him.

The other club which Emerson joined, in fact helped organize, was far different from the Social Circle. Called at first the Symposium, it became known to outsiders as the Transcendental Club and is far better known under that name. Its members were not the sturdy citizens of Concord but intellectual men and women who had been struck by Emerson's ideas, who shared his beliefs, and who recognized him as the head of the new Transcendental movement—a position to which Emerson himself made no claim.

There was little that was practical about any of these people. They were dreamers, idealists, "philosophers," talkers. Only one, Thoreau, was a native of Concord. Several of the most prominent, like Alcott and William Ellery Channing, had moved to Concord for the sole purpose of living near Ralph Waldo Emerson. Other members of this club, which met mostly at Emerson's, sometimes in Elizabeth Peabody's Boston bookshop, came from Boston or nearby towns. A number of them, like Emerson, had been Unitarian ministers. A few still were.

Nucleus of the Transcendental Club was the group which physically and intellectually were closest to Emerson. The group included Amos Bronson Alcott, Margaret Fuller, and Henry David Thoreau.

Alcott, born in Connecticut, had been a Yankee peddler

in Virginia and North Carolina. He had been a school-teacher in Connecticut and in Pennsylvania before, in 1834, he opened a school of his own in the Masonic Temple in Boston. Alcott's educational ideas were too advanced for the time. An indefatigable and undiscourageable talker, he believed in the conversational method of question and answer, as his idol, Plato, had used it in the Socratic dialogues. He tried to teach his child students to think independently, to question, and to find out for themselves, even in moral and religious matters.

As a result, he and his methods were severely attacked by the Boston press. Attendance at his school dropped two-thirds. Alcott fell into debt again. The school's library and its furniture were sold at auction in 1837. The anti-slavery, vegetarian, temperance Alcott, who had only to hear of some new reform to be enthusiastically and loquaciously in favor of it, managed somehow to keep his school going until 1839. In 1840 he gave up and moved to Concord. Emerson had already spoken out in defense of his views. He knew he had a friend there.

Already equipped with three of the four daughters made famous by the second of them, Louisa May Alcott, in *Little Women,* he rented the Hosmer cottage for $30 a year and proposed to support himself and his family by farming the one acre of ground that went with it. Alcott failed at his miniature farming as he failed at all of his practical, money-earning ventures. Alcott spoke well and continually; he wrote continually and very badly. Emerson liked him, found his conversation inspiriting, his prose impossible, and his verse worse.

Margaret Fuller was as driving and determined as Alcott was visionary and scattered in his efforts. Daughter of a congressman, brought up in Cambridge knowing many of the intellectual leaders of Boston and Harvard, she was precocious and intense. She became a teacher, a literary critic, and a bluestocking—a strong upholder of women's rights. Like Alcott, she was a talker. From 1839 to 1844 she held formal "Conversations" in the parlor of Elizabeth Peabody's home in Boston. These gave her a great reputation with the intellectual women of the city. A partial invalid, emotionally and almost abnormally demanding of others, Sarah Margaret Fuller impressed her strong personality on Emerson, Thoreau, and others who worked closely with her.

Married to Margaret Fuller's sister, Ellen, was William Ellery Channing, nephew and namesake of the liberal clergyman and writer Reverend William Ellery Channing. The younger Channing, son of a doctor who was a professor in the Harvard Medical School, fled Harvard to become a romantic poet. He went first to Illinois, where he tried to write poetry as he farmed. Weeding and writing did not weld. Channing gave up the farming and went to Cincinnati where he taught school, studied law, and did some newspaper writing. In 1842 he married Ellen Fuller and moved to Concord to be near Emerson, who had read and praised some of his early verse.

If Alcott was impractical, Channing was improbable. His will-o'-the-wisp nature made it impossible for him to light long enough to fasten on anything securely. He loved nature, waited for inspiration, refused to rewrite and rework his verses, talked wittily and nimbly, was moody, irresponsible, whimsical, and probably as delightful as his verse was horrendous. Channing was Emerson's disciple, but he was Henry Thoreau's companion, just as Henry Thoreau was Emerson's chosen protégé.

Henry David Thoreau was a very different kettle of fish from any other kettle of fish at all. Of French, English, and Scottish ancestry, he had been born in Concord, grown up there, and returned there after his graduation from Harvard in 1837. He had been deeply influenced by Emerson. What Emerson said and wrote, Thoreau also said and wrote, but he was far too original a man and writer to be a mere imitator. Some conclusions which Emerson reached, Thoreau, fourteen years younger, had already reached himself. Other Emersonian ideas and precepts he adopted and made his own.

What Emerson preached, Thoreau practiced. In "The American Scholar" Emerson had told young men to think and act independently. Thoreau acted and thought independently. Emerson preached "Trust thyself." Thoreau trusted himself and no other. Emerson had advised young men not to submit to the world but to let the world come around to them. Thoreau took the advice literally. He did not submit, even though the world showed no signs of coming around in a hurry. Thoreau was tough-minded, independent, and unmalleable.

He fascinated Emerson, who saw great literary promise in the younger man. Thoreau, a woodsman and a craftsman, knew nature as none of the others knew it. He knew it intimately, as a hunter knows it, as the Indians he admired knew it. He gave up schoolteaching after a brief trial to live life as he wished to live it, making his wants few and simple, satisfying them by the efforts of his own hands, and devoting all the rest of his time to being what Emerson had described as "Man Thinking." Henry Thoreau was his own man. Emerson saw that, just as he also saw the reflection of his own thoughts and feelings.

Emerson came to look on the young Thoreau, who was as skilled with his hands as with his mind, as skilled with words as he was with ax or hoe, as "the Man of Concord." In 1848 he took Thoreau into his own home and family for two years. Thoreau, who received his board and room for working in the garden and doing what chores he wished about the house, was the companion of the Emerson children. When Emerson was at home, he and Thoreau worked together in the garden. When he was away lecturing, Thoreau was the man of the house. "One reader and friend of yours dwells now in my house," Emerson wrote Carlyle,

". . . a poet of whom you may one day be proud,—a noble, manly youth, full of melodies and inventions."

Other members of the Transcendental Club were: Theodore Parker, who had been a Unitarian minister; George Ripley, a Unitarian minister who became a literary critic; Orestes Brownson, who had been first a Presbyterian, then a Universalist, then a Unitarian minister, finally a Roman Catholic; William Henry Channing, a Unitarian minister who was another nephew of the older Channing; the poet Jones Very; C. P. Cranch and James Freeman Clarke, both Unitarian ministers.

Ministers or ex-ministers as so many of the members of the Transcendental Club were, they were also writers and editors. Brownson edited *The Boston Quarterly Review,* later the *Democratic Review.* Clarke edited *The Western Messenger.* Parker was to edit *The Massachusetts Quarterly Review.* George Ripley edited the *Christian Register,* then, when he was president of Brook Farm, *The Harbinger.* W. H. Channing, who had edited *The Western Messenger* while he held a pastorate in Cincinnati, was to edit *The Present* and *The Spirit of the Age.* All of them wrote, some prolifically, books and articles in favor of liberal religious thought and reform principles.

Elizabeth Peabody, who had been Alcott's assistant in his Boston school, was also a member of the Club. Her sister, Sophia, had married Nathaniel Hawthorne. Probably it was in this way that Hawthorne, shy and solitary, became a member of the group. Never an avowed Transcendentalist, he was often amused at what he considered the rather farfetched ideas and actions of some of the more enthusiastic adherents of the romantic new attitude.

Hawthorne and his bride had moved into the Old Manse in Concord in 1842. He and Emerson came to know and respect each other. It pleased Hawthorne that he was writing his dark tales of Puritan New England—"The Birthmark," "Young Goodman Brown," "Drowne's Wooden

Image," "Roger Malvin's Burial," and the others—in the same snug study where Emerson had written *Nature*. In the long introduction to *Mosses from an Old Manse,* Hawthorne described the ancestral Emerson home by the battlefield and the river, which flowed past so slowly, Hawthorne said, that it was three weeks before he noticed which way the current flowed. Then he talked of Emerson.

Young visionaries and aged theorists, everyone who came on a new thought, or one he believed was new, made long pilgrimages to Concord to meet Emerson face to face. They besieged him with fads and fancies. They begged his encouragement. They sought his help in all kinds of reform causes. Poets and thinkers, geniuses and crackpots were all attracted by what Hawthorne saw as the wonderful magnetism of Emerson's mind on other minds with like interests.

As is usual with such intellectual and literary groups, the Transcendental Club felt that it needed its own publication, a periodical that would express and broadcast its ideas. After long planning, *The Dial,* so named by Alcott, appeared for the first time in July 1840. Margaret Fuller was its editor. George Ripley was her assistant.

The new quarterly, appearing in July, October, January, and April, 136 pages in each issue, was subtitled: "A Magazine for Literature, Philosophy, and Religion." In "The American Scholar" Emerson had urged a native American culture and original writing by talented American writers. In *The Dial* he wanted to give such writers, Alcott, Fuller, Channing, and particularly Thoreau, a chance to be published and read. That was his chief interest in the periodical.

The first page of the first *Dial* said that the new magazine was published in obedience to a strong current of thought and feeling "which, for a few years past, has led many sincere persons in New England to make new demands on literature, and to reprobate the rigor of our

Emerson, Margaret Fuller, and Henry Thoreau edited The Dial.

conventions of religion and education which is turning us to stone, which renounces hope, which looks only backward, which asks only such a future as the past, which suspects improvement, and holds nothing so much in horror as new views and the dreams of youth." Evidently it was Margaret Fuller's firm intention to change all this.

All but one of the contributions to the first number of *The Dial* were unsigned. Thoreau's poem "Sympathy," which had brought about his introduction to Emerson, was initialed "T," as was his prose essay on Aulus Persius Flaccus. Emerson's poem "The Problem" was not even initialed. Only Bronson Alcott's name was blazoned on the first fifty of his "Orphic Sayings." These were sentences or short paragraphs on such subjects as enthusiasm, prudence, hope, immortality, discontent, speech, character, and aspiration. The first part of an anonymous serial, "Ernest the Seeker," was run. The issue ended with a filler bit, obviously from the pen of Margaret Fuller, which sounds rather affected and silly now. "Did you never admire anything your friend did merely because he did it? Never!—you always had a better reason. Wise man, you never knew what it is to love."

Almost all of the members of the Transcendental Club contributed to *The Dial*. Another of Thoreau's early poems, "Sic Vita," was in the second issue. Originally he had wrapped it about a bunch of violets and tossed it to Mrs. Lucy Brown, a sister of Emerson's wife, when she was a boarder in his mother's home. Thoreau appeared in prose or verse in almost every *Dial*. Channing's rapturous and sentimental verse was in most issues. Ripley, Cranch, and Parker all had their say. More of Emerson's best poems, "Forbearance," "Woodnotes," "The Sphinx," "The Park," "Fate," appeared in various issues. There were more blocks of Alcott's portentous "Orphic Sayings." There were articles on art, music, religion, always plenty of verse, and numerous book reviews.

Her editorship of *The Dial* was Margaret Fuller's first venture into journalism, and she responded eagerly to the challenge. For two years, imperious, dictatorial, but intent and in many ways capable, she worked hard at it. Many of the reviews she wrote herself. The position of women in the world, man *vs.* woman, was a favorite subject, and she gave it plenty of space.

When George Ripley disappeared into his enthusiasm for Brook Farm and then went to head the idyllic community when it was established in West Roxbury, Thoreau took over as Margaret Fuller's assistant. He suffered under her criticism, which was often just, learned much, and worked away at the periodical which, though it could not pay its contributors, gave him an incentive to write and was making his name known.

Though he was allowed to sign his material and was given more space than most of the others, Bronson Alcott was dissatisfied. *The Dial* for April 1842 contained not only still another block of his "Orphic Sayings" but also a letter to the editor. He asked for the return of a rejected manuscript, then said, "The Dial prefers a style of thought and diction, not mine; nor can I add to its popularity with its chosen readers. A fit organ for such as myself is not yet, but is to be."

Alcott was not the only dissatisfied reader of *The Dial*. The popular press seldom approves of the "little magazine." The literary little magazine always represents the thought or the literary manner of a cultural minority. Usually it is well written, and obviously it is noncommercial. Its writers are seldom well known. Often they are young and demanding change from comfortably established ways. When the newspapers and the larger magazines deign to notice a little magazine at all, it is usually with indignant alarm and the virtuous intention of stamping it out.

As Emerson wrote Carlyle, *The Dial* was viciously attacked by almost every newspaper and magazine. It was ridiculed and derided. It was accused of being too feminine—which under Margaret Fuller it was. It was accused of being irreligious, which it was not. *The Dial,* said the enraged writers and editors who struck at it, was edited by zanies and bedlamites. Alcott, an easy target, was particularly singled out for parody and contemptuous comment. Though he knew its shortcomings and wished it were better, Emerson told Carlyle that he thought *The Dial* was serving a useful purpose, particularly for the young writers he wished to encourage, and he was anxious for the magazine to continue.

Carlyle thought that Emerson should forget *The Dial* and get on with his more important writing. Emerson was doing that too.

With Thoreau attending to his gardens and other household chores, with the Social Circle and the Transcendental Club providing relaxation and stimulus, with Walden Pond and the woods and fields of Concord a continual delight and inspiration, Emerson was hard at work in his study.

Often Waldo played about his feet as he wrote. When the boy was two years old, he built a tower of two spools, a card, an awl case, and a flower box. When she came into the study, Lidian was so transported with her son's architectural achievement that she fell to the floor and kissed it, then rushed off to see Waldo, who by this time was in his nursery.

Waldo was three when Emerson wrote in his journal, "I like my boy, with his endless, sweet soliloquies and iterations, and his utter inability to conceive why I should not leave all my nonsense business and writing, and come to tie up his toy horse."

The next summer Emerson worried that Waldo looked thin. He seemed to be all eyes and eyelashes. Waldo worried about him too. One day when he saw his father working clumsily with a shovel in his garden, he cried out, "Look out, Papa! You will dig your leg!"

In the winter of 1840 Emerson delivered a course of ten lectures in Boston. His general subject was "The Present Age." After an introductory lecture, he spoke twice on literature, then on politics, private life, reforms, religion, ethics, educations, and tendencies. He read the lectures on ten consecutive Wednesday evenings to audiences that averaged about four hundred on each occasion. The lectures were well received, but Emerson was not satisfied. He spent about twenty-one hours preparing each lecture. He wished he could spend sixty.

No matter what he called a lecture, Emerson always spoke on one subject. He knew this. On April 7, 1840, he wrote in his journal, "In all my lectures, I have taught one doctrine, namely, the infinitude of the private man. This the people accept readily enough, and even with loud commendation, as long as I call the lecture Art, or Politics, or Literature, or the Household; but the moment I call it Religion, they are shocked, though it be only the application of the same truth which they receive everywhere else, to a new class of facts."

Emerson was doing more than working on his lectures now. He was cutting and shaping, rewriting and tightening material from these lectures into the first book of his essays. He was writing with extreme care, pondering every sentence, every word, every phrase, cutting to achieve the terseness he wished. He allowed no word to remain in the final draft that did not carry its own weight and force. He sent the completed manuscript to his publishers early in 1841.

Emerson knew what he wanted the book to accomplish. "I would have my book read," he noted after its appearance, "as I have read my favorite books, not with explosion and astonishment, a marvel and a rocket, but a friendly and

87

agreeable influence stealing like the scent of a flower, or the sight of a new landscape on a traveller. I wish neither to be hated and defied by such as I startle, nor to be kissed and hugged by the young whose thoughts I stimulate."

Essays, First Series was published in the spring of 1841.

6

Emerson's *Essays* is one of the truly American books for which he had pleaded in "The American Scholar." It is more than that. It is one of the world's original books, known and read wherever men and women can read and think. With its publication in 1841, Emerson was immediately recognized, in England as well as in the United States, as a thinker and writer, the foremost American writer of that time and for a long time afterward.

A few hundred people could hear Emerson lecture. A few hundred more had read *Nature*, "The American Scholar," "The Divinity School Address," and such of his prose and verse as *The Dial* or other of the little magazines had published. The *Essays* took Emerson to a national, then to an international public.

The essays are far less difficult to read than *Nature*. The sentences are shorter and more memorable. They have a harder, polished brilliance. They are clearer, more forceful. Emerson had pruned and pared his reflections, then phrased them into telling aphorisms that read sometimes almost like proverbs or maxims. Yet the essays tell the same story he had told before and was to tell again. The essays, whatever their various titles, are about the one subject he talked about in all his lectures, "the infinitude of the private man," that is, the limitless possibilities in every individual. In the essays Emerson told again, but in words that could be read and reread, of the importance of every man and woman and of the unity of their souls with nature and with God.

The *Essays* published in 1841 were twelve in number: their subjects were History, Self-Reliance, Compensation, Spiritual Laws, Love, Friendship, Prudence, Heroism, The Over-Soul, Circles, Intellect, and Art. These essays were Emerson crystallized. They said all that he was and meant. This was his first complete letter to the world.

Best known, perhaps, and certainly the most characteristic of all the essays in this first volume is "Self-Reliance." It contains many of the most familiar and most often quoted sentences and passages from Emerson. Here is part of the Emersonian wisdom that has become part of the world's wisdom.

Trust thyself: every heart vibrates to that iron string.

There is a time in every man's education when he arrives at the conviction that envy is ignorance; that imitation is suicide; that he must take himself for better for worse as his portion . . .

Whoso would be a man, must be a nonconformist.

No law can be sacred to me but that of my own nature.

There is a class of persons to whom by all spiritual affinity I am bought and sold; for them I will go to prison if need be; but your miscellaneous popular charities; the education at college of fools; the building of meeting-houses to the vain end to which many now stand; alms to sots; and the thousand-fold Relief Societies;—though I confess with shame I sometimes succumb and give the dollar, it is a wicked dollar, which by and by I shall have the manhood to withhold.

It is easy in the world to live after the world's opinion; it is easy in solitude to live after our own; but the great man is he who in the midst of the crowd keeps with perfect sweetness the independence of solitude.

A foolish consistency is the hobgoblin of little minds . . . Speak what you think now in hard words and to-morrow speak what to-morrow thinks in hard words again, though it contradict every thing you said today. . . . The voyage of the best ship is a zigzag of a hundred tacks. See the line from a sufficient distance, and it straightens itself to the average tendency.

An institution is the lengthened shadow of one man . . .

. . . the essence of genius, of virtue, and of life, [is that] which we call Spontaneity or Instinct. We denote this primary wisdom as Intuition, whilst all later teachings are tuitions.

If we live truly, we shall see truly. It is as easy for the strong man to be strong, as it is for the weak to be weak.

God is here within.

Insist on yourself; never imitate.

There is mysticism in the *Essays,* but none of the mistiness of *Nature.* Instead of penning abstruse reflections, Emerson spoke now in bold, hard-hitting words whose meaning, sentence by sentence, is inescapable. There is a four-square, no-nonsense muscularity in his directness. Emerson meant what he said, and he knew how to say it.

It was a foolish consistency Emerson condemned in "Self-Reliance." In all of his writing he showed a consistency, a uniformity of thought and statement, that was not so much a conscious device as the unity, the integrity, that emerges when a man is truly himself. It was the unconscious expression of not a foolish but a sane and inescapable consistency which was peculiarly Emerson's. Whatever his subject, whether it was history, art, compensation, or the Over-Soul, Emerson spoke about the same things—the limitless possibilities in the individual, the identity of the individual's soul with that of the universe, and the participation of one man's soul in the combined soul of all people.

Like Carlyle, Emerson saw history as the lives of the great men who made it. In his essay "History" he wrote that properly there is no history, only biography. He adopted the same position toward history that he had adopted toward miracles in his "Divinity School Address." In that address he had said that miracles are not only of the past; the miracle of life is now, in the present. In the essay he wrote, "I have no expectation that any man will read history aright who thinks that what was done in a remote age, by men whose names have resounded far, has any deeper sense than what he is doing to-day."

In one of his finest poems, "The Rhodora," Emerson wrote that "Beauty is its own excuse for being." Beauty needs no other reason for its existence. In his essay on "Art" he said much the same thing. Art, he said, is at one with nature, and we carry our own appreciation of beauty wherever we are and wherever we go. Real genius, he said, which expresses itself in art, has nothing to do with the merely decorative. Just as we have an inborn appreciation of beauty, art, through the intuition and awareness of the artist, pierces directly through to the simple, the beautiful, and the true.

When he spoke of "Heroism," Emerson was as consistent as when he talked about history or art. For him heroism, too, was based on self-reliance. "Heroism is an

obedience to a secret impulse of an individual's character.
. . . Self-trust is the essence of heroism."

In both *Nature* and "The Divinity School Address"
Emerson had touched upon the subject he develops in the
essay on "the Over-Soul." By "Over-Soul" he meant, in
his own words, "that Unity . . . within which every man's
particular being is contained and made one with all other."
The soul of every man or woman, distinct and complete
in itself, is also part of the whole soul of universal man
and woman.

The soul, Emerson said, is neither an organ nor a func-
tion. It is not intellect or will, not mind or intent, but more
than all of these. It is a force which controls both mind
and purpose in man. It is a light which shines through
every human being. "When it breathes through his intellect, it is genius; when it breathes through his will, it is
virtue; when it flows through his affections, it is love."

Then, as he so often does, Emerson tightened what he
had explained at length into one terse, unforgettable figure
of speech: "Jove nods to Jove behind each of us."

It was Emerson's habit to preface his essays with poems
or passages of verse, sometimes quoted but more often of
his own writing. These contain the essence of the idea
which he expands in the prose of his essay. They are
poems, not arithmetical explanations, and they must be
read as poems which intimate more than they can say in
a-b-c fashion. Yet the verses he placed before "Compensation," perhaps the most difficult of the 1841 *Essays,* are
a fair guide to his thought in the essay.

> The wings of Time are black and white,
> Pied with morning and with night.
> Mountain tall and ocean deep
> Trembling balance duly keep.
> In changing moon, in tidal wave,
> Glows the feud of Want and Have. . . .

It is a mistaken notion, Emerson says in "Compensation," that justice is meted out in the hereafter. Justice is here and now and in the very nature of things. Everything in nature, he pointed out, is a part of something else. Everything is a half which suggests something else to make it whole. There is a balance in all things: man, woman; odd, even; in, out; upper, under; yes, no. Every gift is balanced or compensated for by its accompanying defect. For everything you get, you lose something. For everything you lose, you gain something else.

"Every excess causes a defect; every defect an excess. Every sweet hath its sour; every evil its good. . . . For every thing you have missed, you have gained something else; and for everything you gain, you lose something." That is the balance. That is the compensation.

The farmer, Emerson says, envies the President his place and power, but the President has usually paid dearly for his White House. "It has commonly cost him all his peace, and the best of his manly attributes." Retribution is inherent in every act. If laws are too severe, juries will not convict. Pain will result from overindulgence in pleasure. Then, as so often in Emerson, comes the terse image that says it all:

The dice of God are always loaded.

For Emerson, of course, the answer is self-trust. The man who acts in accordance with his own best instincts and impulses will attain the compensation, receive the justice, that is inherent in the very nature of this law of balance. Compensation for the seeming inequality of earthly rewards lies in the nature of the soul.

"Compensation" contains one of the finest and most poetic passages in all Emerson. It cannot be analyzed as a compound can be analyzed in a chemistry laboratory. It cannot be translated into an algebraic formula. Yet it comes very close to stating in strong imagery the idea which possessed Emerson, the idea, it can almost be said, which he was.

> There is a deeper fact in the soul than compensation, to wit, its own nature. The soul is not a compensation but a life. The soul *is*. Under all this running sea of circumstance, whose waters ebb and flow with perfect balance, lies the aboriginal abyss of real Being. Essence, or God, is not a relation, or a part, but the whole.

The 1841 *Essays* is Emerson's great book. Here is his idealism, his ethereality. Here is the very magic of his writing. Here also is the sound common sense of the shrewdly observant man. A vibrant sanity underlies the soaring thought. Emerson knew and appreciated everyday life as well as the realm of thought and spirit into which his vision lifts both him and his reader.

It was this which disturbed some of the Concord inner circle. With the license of intimacy, *The Dial* reviewed the *Essays* in April 1842. Margaret Fuller admitted that the essays were "truly noble," but she complained that they failed to inspire the reviewer. The essays were too intellectual. They were not mystical and emotional enough for the undisciplined minds of the devout romantics among the Transcendentalists.

Emerson would have made his essays even more forthright and direct. Instead of writing in "Self-Reliance" that a foolish consistency is the hobgoblin of little minds, he wished the literary fashions of the day had permitted him to write "Damn consistency!" Profanity, he thought, was sometimes the best and most forceful rhetoric. Emerson always preferred the strongest word. He wished, he said, that the stinging dialect of the sailor could be domesticated. He got no satisfaction from literary meetings. The talk of those who considered themselves literary men was always muddy. Emerson preferred a rattling oath from a teamster or a drover. The speech of such men was brief, brisk, and to the point compared with a serious page in one of the solemn literary magazines. The truckman's profanity was sound. "Cut these words and they would bleed; they are vascular and alive; they walk and run."

Emerson saw men and women doing hard work as he went back and forth to the city. The North Boston streets were full of them. Their movements and actions were strong. Their dress and manners were rough, yet these people were the material of real art, for there was blood and bone and heart in them. He preferred the picture they made to the picture made by the fashionably dressed ladies and gentlemen in Washington and Tremont Streets.

Ripley, Margaret Fuller, and Alcott were all agog now over their plans for Brook Farm. They expected that the socialistic community in which all would share the work and the rewards and stimulate each other through high thinking, conversation, and writing would cure all the world's ills, their own in particular. It would be all one big ambrosial family at Brook Farm. They expected Emerson's enthusiastic agreement and support. They did not get it.

Emerson tried. He wanted to be convinced. He tried to melt and be inflamed by the enthusiasm of the others. He could not. Neither his common sense nor his belief that a man should work out his own salvation by himself would allow of it.

His own home was far too precious to him for him to feel any real interest in communal schemes. His family was growing as well as his landed estate. Waldo had two sisters now. Ellen, named after his first wife, had been born in February 1839. Edith was born in November 1841.

One day in the late fall of 1841 John Thoreau came by the Emerson's, where his brother was living. A daguerreotypist, he told Emerson, was in town, and he suggested that it would be a good idea if Waldo had his picture taken. Emerson agreed, and John took the handsome little five-year-old boy to sit for his likeness. Years afterward Emerson remembered how much he had to thank John Thoreau for "that wise and gentle piece of friendship."

Already stricken by tuberculosis, John Thoreau died agonizingly of lockjaw on January 11, 1842. Henry Thoreau was desolate and bitter, for the brothers had been close companions.

Two weeks later Waldo was taken seriously ill with scarlet fever. The disease developed rapidly and the child weakened alarmingly fast. On the morning of January 27 the Alcotts sent one of their daughters to ask how he was. When Louisa May Alcott, who was eight years old, knocked at the door, it was Emerson who let her in. She was so startled at his worn and grief-stricken face that she could only stammer out her message.

"Child, he is dead!" Emerson told her.

The deaths of Ellen, Edward, and Charles had been difficult for Emerson to bear. This was far worse. He had loved and idolized his son. He had no defense against this loss. He could scarcely believe what had happened.

He wrote brief notes telling of Waldo's death to his brother William, to his sister-in-law, Lucy Jackson Brown, to Elizabeth Hoar, who had been like a godmother to Waldo, to Elizabeth Peabody, and to other close friends. He broke down when he wrote his Aunt Mary Moody Emerson. "My boy, my boy is gone. . . . My darling and the world's wonderful child, for never in my own or another family have I seen anything comparable, has fled out of my arms like a dream. He adorned the world for me like a morning star, and every particular of my daily life."

Thoreau, who had loved the child too and sought solace in Waldo for his brother's death, said that Waldo had gone as the mist rises from the brook. Emerson wrote in his journal that Waldo died as a bird gives up his breath. He found comfort in nothing. Two months later he wrote in his journal: "I comprehend nothing of this fact but its

"Child, he is dead!"

98

bitterness. Explanation I have none, consolation none that rises out of the fact itself; only diversion; only oblivion of this, and pursuit of new objects." Two years later he was still unreconciled. The pain had not ceased. He wrote a friend, "I had no experiences nor progresses to reconcile me to the calamity whose anniversary returned the second time last Saturday. Waldo's death."

Emerson and Thoreau, teacher and scholar, patron and protégé, were drawn more closely together by the two deaths which neither could understand or accept. Emerson must have found some comfort in the near presence of the younger man, difficult as he was, whose literary abilities he perceived and fostered. For the rest, he turned to his work.

There were always his lectures to prepare, then deliver. About $800 a year of his income came from these lectures. In Boston he got $50 a lecture. The country lyceums paid him $10 and traveling expenses. Though he was paid more in later years, up to 1847 the largest sum of money he ever received for a series of ten lectures was $570.

Emerson did not despise money as Alcott, to whom he gave often and generously, and many of the other reformers affected to do. He was glad of the extra income which enabled his family to live well—though it did not, as he wrote Carlyle, allow him the luxury of indulging his fancy for even some small objects that might please him. Yet, though he valued his earnings, Emerson was probably more grateful at this point in his life for the relief from pain that absorption in his work afforded him.

He was hard at work preparing a second volume of his essays for publication, and he took on another demanding task.

Margaret Fuller had been promised $200 a year for editing *The Dial*. She was never paid. The magazine's original publisher, Weeks, Jordan and Company of Washington Street in Boston, went bankrupt. Elizabeth Peabody took over the publishing, printing the magazine on a press behind her bookshop at 109 Washington Street. *The Dial,* with only three hundred subscribers, was barely making its expenses.

Having served her apprenticeship and learned her trade, Margaret Fuller resigned and left *The Dial* in 1842 to write a book about a trip to Chicago which she took in 1843. In 1844 she entered the household of Horace Greeley in Chappaqua, New York, and began to write for his *New York Tribune.*

Financially *The Dial* was in a bad way, but Emerson still believed in its usefulness. Rather than suffer the quarterly to expire, he took over the editorship himself, with Thoreau continuing as assistant.

Emerson opened the issue for July 1842 with his own signed "Lectures on the Times." This he followed with a reprint of "The Natural History of Massachusetts," which had just been issued by the Zoological and Botanical Society of the Commonwealth. This was factual, less vague and transcendentally rhapsodic material than Margaret Fuller had used. It is possible that Thoreau had a part in its selection.

Emerson made *The Dial* a firmer effort. There was less yearning Victorian poetry, less fulsome prose. He introduced some of the sacred writings of the Orient into its pages, printing "The Preaching of Buddha," extracts from "The White Lotus of the Good Law." In April 1843 he used, unsigned, "A Leaf from 'A Voyage to Porto Rico.'" It was, as edited, a lively account which had been written by his brother Charles. In various issues he used other writing left by the younger brother he had loved. It must have pleased the editor to be able to do this. He gave William Ellery Channing a by-line for his prose tale written as a series of letters, "The Youth of the Poet and the Painter," which began as a serial in July 1843. He continued generously to use some of his own best work in

The Dial and to publish Thoreau, Fuller, Channing, and Alcott.

About this time, Emerson did more for Alcott than merely publish his platitudinous "Orphic Sayings." Alcott, most vocal of the impractical dreamers, was despondent over his various failures. He could not farm, he could not write, he could not do anything well except talk. Yet he was appealing, and the tenderhearted Emerson valued him for his shining goodness and unquenchable optimism.

Alcott had been corresponding with men in England who, sharing the same educational ideas which had brought him disaster in Boston, had founded a school near London and christened it Alcott House. Believing that the trip might help restore his spirits, Emerson gave Alcott $500 and sent him abroad in the spring of 1842.

He provided Alcott with letters of introduction to Carlyle and others he knew, but, knowing his man, he also sent Alcott after his arrival there another letter which he ordered him to read to his English friends at Alcott House. The letter said that they could safely trust Alcott's theories but warned them that they could trust his statements of fact not at all.

Despite this, when Alcott returned to Concord he brought with him Charles Lane and Lane's young son, William. All living together in the Alcott home in Concord, they laid plans for still another Utopian community. They bought a farm of one hundred acres near the village of Harvard.

More charitable than usual, Carlyle had written Emerson after meeting Alcott that he liked him. No one, he said, could laugh at Alcott without loving him. He also said that Alcott seemed "all bent on saving the world by a return to acorns and the golden age."

The Alcott family, the Lanes, and a dozen disciples did not live on acorns at Fruitlands, as they named their community, but they came as close to it as they could. They ate no meat or fish. They did without eggs, milk, cheese, and butter because cows and hens should not be enslaved. For the same reason they used no horses on the farm. They could not use manure to fertilize the ground because they considered that would be unspiritual. The amateur farmers planted late and poorly that spring, but they led a happy and idyllic existence that summer. Emerson, who visited Fruitlands then, wrote in his journal, "They look well in July. We will see them in December."

Emerson's dubiousness was justified. At harvest time the men of the community were away attending a meeting of one of the numerous reform groups they favored. With a storm threatening, Mrs. Alcott and the girls gathered in what crops they could. As the cold weather came on, most of the outsiders who had hopefully joined in the venture vanished. By midwinter only the Lanes and Alcott and his long-suffering wife and four daughters remained. Finally the heroes decided against cold and starvation, and the project broke up in quarrels and bitterness.

For a time the Alcotts lived with a farmer, and Alcott chopped wood for their keep. Then Mrs. Alcott and Emerson came to the rescue. Mrs. Alcott inherited almost enough money from her father to purchase a new home. Emerson gave her the additional $500 they needed, and the Alcotts returned once more to Concord and an old house about a third of a mile from Emerson's on the road to Lexington.

The Dial for April 1844 contained an article, "Life in the Woods," by Charles Lane. Its author still favored raw nature over city civilization. He argued that the woods were always better for soul and body than all the ills which resulted from city and town living. The woods exalted the spirit, he said. The article had been written before the breakup of Fruitlands, but even then Lane had begun to suspect that all was not perfect. He had to admit that by the time the nature dweller had chopped his wood and baked his bread, milked the cows and cleaned out the barn, planted and hoed and weeded, he had neither time nor energy left for writing lyric poetry and thinking inspired thoughts.

Another article in this same *Dial* was about Immanuel Kant, the great German thinker. The article credited him with having forwarded the leading idea of Transcendentalism, the idea that people can have direct, subjective knowledge of truths; that is, that they can know things that it is not possible to see and hear, or to taste, smell, or touch, and thus understand. At the time Emerson did not know the young author of this article. It was James Elliot Cabot, whom many years later he was to look upon almost as a younger brother, and whom he was to choose to edit his manuscripts and whom the family would select to write his life story.

Toward the back of this *Dial* for April 1844 was "The Young American," a long lecture of twenty-three pages signed R. W. Emerson. It had been given before the Mercantile Library Association in Boston, February 7, 1844. It looked as if the editor was using what material he had readily at hand. There was no other indication that this was to be the last issue of *The Dial*. It was.

The Dial had never been all that Emerson had hoped it would be. He offered no excuses. The most famous little magazine in the history of American letters had run its course for four years. Despite all its faults, it had provided its contributors with a forum while they prepared for the later literary accomplishments which many of them, notably Thoreau, achieved.

Emerson relinquished his editorship with great relief. "You will think me, O much performing friend, the spoiled child of luxury if I should tell you how gay to me is the prospect of liberation from the Dial and how pleasant is the promise of the literary labours before me, when this is gone," he wrote the absent Margaret Fuller. "One would think it was the American Encyclopedia that was in hand & not our poor little pamphlet."

Emerson had done his best for Alcott. Unlike Alcott, Thoreau could write, and his job as "private secretary to the President of the Dial," as Emerson jestingly called it, was over. Emerson's faith in Thoreau's ability was still as strong as his affection for the thorny individualist who lived in his house, did his chores, and showed no signs of seeking more conventional occupation.

His own burning ambitions as a younger man made it hard for Emerson to understand what seemed to be Thoreau's total lack of any ambition at all. In Concord he had already done everything he could think of to help advance Thoreau. He decided that now he would try to give Henry his chance at success in the larger world where his talents might be recognized.

Emerson arranged with his brother William to take Thoreau into his home on Staten Island, New York, as tutor to his children. It is unlikely that the William Emersons were in dire need of a tutor; likely that William, Emerson, and Thoreau himself all knew this. Emerson's real purpose was to make Thoreau acquainted with the literary world of New York and known to the writers and editors, like Henry James and Horace Greeley, who might help further his career.

Busy with his own affairs, his lecturing, his accounts, his correspondence, with arranging for halls in which to speak and having advance advertisements prepared, with doing his part in looking after his retarded brother Bulkeley, Emerson strove to do his best for Thoreau. It was agreed that William Emerson would take Thoreau into his home much as Emerson had taken him into his. This time, though, Thoreau's particular task would be to guide and instruct Willie Emerson, not just as to his spelling and arithmetic, but the whole boy. For this, Thoreau was to have his board, lodging, a room to study in—the room to have a fire when needed—and one hundred dollars for a year.

Home again after long travels on the lecture circuit, Emerson wrote his brother, March 12, 1843, that Thoreau thought this would fit him. Dryly he added, ". . . & he very rarely finds offers that do fit him." Thoreau, who had been unwell, felt he could do no manual work. He wanted to know whether there was any clerical work from William's law office or from any other office which would enable him to add a bit more to his income. Thoreau thought, Emerson told his brother, that he could make his rather careless handwriting legible enough.

A month later Thoreau had tightened his terms. He wanted to be certain that in winter he would have a heated room available to him alone for reading, writing, and declaiming in. Thoreau had always had such a luxury and insisted upon it. Could not William use the basement evenings and Thoreau the library, or the reverse? Evidently William agreed to the new demands, and Thoreau left for Staten Island in May 1843.

Just as he differed from those surrounding him in kind and degree of character and ability—an original thinker and writer among men of anything from marked talent to mere good will—Emerson differed from them in other ways. He lived with common sense, calm grace, and hard work. Where Alcott, Thoreau, and Channing avoided responsibilities, Emerson sought them. Where they abstained from distasteful effort, Emerson welcomed it. With lesser gifts, they were forced to hoard their energies and talents. Emerson spent freely.

The second volume of his *Essays* was published in 1844.

Essays, Second Series dealt with more temporal matters than the first series published three years earlier. The essays are less about the abstract and ideal and more about the practical and factual. The shrewdly observant Emerson is more evident than the poet and mystic. Except in his essay on the poet, his style is harder and more matter-of-fact. Emerson's subjects this time were: The Poet, Experience, Character, Manners, Gifts, Nature, Politics, Nominalist and Realist, and New England Reformers.

The poet, said Emerson, is the sayer, the namer. He stands for the love of beauty. He sees and knows and tells what other men do not see as clearly and cannot name or tell until he has shown and told them.

Character is the latent force in a man, a reserve over and above talent and ability. It is unseen but is somehow communicated to others. Emerson saw character as self-sufficiency.

In "Manners" Emerson defined the gentleman as a man of force, then of gentleness. He is composed and independent, at home in whatever society he finds himself. The gentleman has original energy. "In politics and in trade, bruisers and pirates are of better promise than talkers or clerks. . . . My gentleman gives the law wherever he is; he will outpray saints in chapel, outgeneral veterans in the field, and outshine all courtesy in the hall. He is good company for pirates and good with academicians . . ."

This is a more worldly and sharp-spoken Emerson in the second series of his essays. In "New England Reformers" he said that men felt a growing distrust of organizations and institutions such as business, government, education, and the Church, and that there was a growing trust in the self-supplied capabilities of the private individual. For this reason he had little faith in Utopian communities such as Fruitlands and Brook Farm. The strong, he said, made themselves self-sufficient; the weak acted in concert and withdrew from the world into their dream communities in order to indulge and enjoy their particular fads and fancies. He was sharply ironic about such goings-on.

What a fertility of projects for the salvation of the world! One apostle thought all men should go to farming, and another that no man should buy or sell, that the use of money was the cardinal evil; another that the mischief was in our diet, that we eat and drink damnation. These made unleavened bread and were foes to the death to fermentation. . . . Others attacked . . . the use of animal manures in farming, and the tyranny of man over brute nature; . . . The ox must be taken from the plough and the horse from the cart. . . . Even the insect world was to be defended,— that had been too long neglected, and a society for the protection of ground-worms, slugs and mosquitoes was to be incorporated without delay.

Emerson had had enough of reformers and their hobby-horses that they tried to ride like chargers. Their communities did not draw the able and the good. Men of energy and independence of spirit preferred, as he preferred, to take their chances in the world and to make their own way as best they could.

Neither was Emerson the blind adherent of democracy or of any other form of government. He made that very clear in "Politics," where he wrote, "Every actual State is corrupt. Good men must not obey the laws too well. What satire on government can equal the severity of censure conveyed in the world *politic,* which now for ages has signified *cunning,* intimating that the State is a trick?"

With Thomas Jefferson, Emerson believed the less government the better. He admitted the necessity of having some form of government and said that human nature expressed itself in making laws just as much as in carving statues or writing songs or building railroads, and he said that the laws of nations are really an expression of the common human conscience. Yet he noted this too:

A man who cannot be acquainted with me, taxes me; looking from afar at me ordains that a part of my labor shall go to this or that whimsical end,—not as I, but as he happens to fancy. Behold the consequence. Of all debts men are least willing to pay the taxes. What a satire is this on government! Everywhere they think they get their money's worth, except for these.

Rather than government imposed from without, Emerson, as always, favored rule imposed from within by the individual's own mind and conscience. Nothing good, he said, can be expected from political parties. Everything good can be expected from the influence of private character, of the sincere man acting with dignity and good will toward his fellows. Emerson believed that self-government should supersede the government of external force and restraint.

A nation of friends, he thought, could build roads, carry letters, and guarantee each man the fruits of his own labors better than a government which enforces its will by threats of punishment and the use of police force. Emerson was not naïve. He did not expect the immediate abolition of armed, restrictive government. As long as men are selfish and pursue only their selfish ends, there will always be such a government. When men become wiser and outgrow their selfishness, it will no longer be necessary.

Present methods, he suggested mildly, are not so excellent that better ones may not be considered. "The power of love, as the basis of the State, has never been tried."

7

Emerson liked to walk with Thoreau, who, like Alcott, was soon back in Concord living in his family's home. Thoreau knew the woods, fields, and streams like a fox or an otter. He seemed to know every tree and flower. Either he knew the language of the birds and beasts or they knew his. A walk with Thoreau was often a bright revelation to Emerson.

Thoreau could tramp the day long without tiring. Emerson was hardly a novice at walking. In the summer of 1823, when he was twenty, he had walked the forty miles from Roxbury to Worcester without difficulty in one day. Then he had walked into western Massachusetts, through Brookfield and Palmer to Ware to Belchertown. From Belchertown a few days later he had walked to Amherst, where he attended the first commencement of "the infant college" in the Connecticut Valley. The college, he noted for some reason, was supposed to have a net worth of $85,000.

Emerson walked with Thoreau, and he walked about Concord with Ellery Channing and Bronson Alcott. These were strolls merely, with animated conversation usually more important to his companions than the free movement of their legs. Emerson usually preferred to walk alone. He believed in walking. "When you have worn out your shoes," he told his son, "the strength of the shoe-leather has gone into the fibre of your body." Carrying a heavy suitcase, Emerson could walk across a city to his train so fast that companions had almost to run to keep up.

One fine September day in 1842 Emerson and Nathaniel Hawthorne set out for a walk. They were in fine spirits and, for once—for Hawthorne seldom talked and Emerson was more apt to listen than to speak—their conversation was easy and free. The essayist and poet and the writer of imaginative tales and romances were the two men of greatest stature and literary accomplishment of all the Concord group and only a year apart in age.

They ate their noon meal at an unattractive inn, Emerson complaining that the Temperance Society had emptied the taverns where a traveler could once share in the jokes and political talk of teamsters and farmers. Having dined at Stow, they continued their tramp toward the village of Harvard. They walked twenty miles that day, though the last two miles they got a lift in a wagon driven by an old gentleman who had known of Emerson's father. He drove them right to the tavern and bade the landlord look after them well.

The two left Harvard at half past six the next morning and walked three and a half miles to a Shaker village, where they breakfasted. These Shakers, Emerson decided, were neither worldly nor stupid like some others he had seen. After a good breakfast, they walked on to Littleton, thence to Acton. They reached Concord before four o'clock on the afternoon of the second day, having hiked another nineteen miles.

This was a happy interlude which Emerson enjoyed in the bitter year of Waldo's death. He valued Hawthorne. He valued all his Concord neighbors, but he was a realist in his private judgment of his fellows. He did not value

Emerson and Nathaniel Hawthorne went for a forty-mile walk in 1842.

111

Hawthorne's writing highly and thought his reputation as a writer was a tribute to the man, "because his writing is not good for anything." When Elizabeth Peabody, the novelist's sister-in-law, lent him Hawthorne's *Footprints on the Seashore,* he complained that there was no inside to the book. Hawthorne and Alcott, he decided, put together would make one man.

Smiling and courteous, always a little aloof, always generous in his attempts to help them, Emerson kept his opinions of his friends to himself but sometimes entered sharp and satirical comments in his journal.

Alcott, who often carried a small bronze bust of Plato in his pocket, hoping it would inspire him, was pathetic. He was really a well-intentioned bore. Emerson called him a "tedious archangel," again, "an innocent charlatan." Alcott had nobility of nature, serenity of deportment, but he was a sloppy workman and, worse in Emerson's eyes, an incompetent writer. "He never quotes; he never refers; his only illustration is his own biography. His topic yesterday is Alcott on the 17th October; today, Alcott on the 18th October; tomorrow, on the 19th." Emerson tried to be fair in a long entry in his journal in 1842, but his impatience and annoyance show sharply through.

Two years later Emerson wrote that Alcott, "the magnificent dreamer," who had been rejected everywhere, was just as optimistic as when he began. "Very pathetic it is to see this wandering Emperor from year to year making his rounds of visits from house to house of such as do not exclude him, seeking a companion, tired of pupils."

The Alcotts were always poor, often in need. When he called, it was Emerson's habit to leave a ten-dollar or twenty-dollar bill tucked under a picture or a vase in the parlor or dining room. He could love, but he could not condone. Alcott, he thought, was like a slate pencil with a sponge tied to the other end. The sponge erased the lines as soon as the pencil drew them. Alcott talked high and happily, then promptly forgot all that he had said. Emerson damned him finally in an annihilating epitaph which he wrote and underlined in his journal in October 1848: *Here lies the Amateur*.

Even with his favorite, Henry Thoreau, Emerson grew impatient and with reason. He told him bluntly that he said nothing new in his writing. The thoughts were Emerson's, dressed out in different words. He had not yet said what he was created to say. A device of Thoreau's writing exasperated him: "The trick of his rhetoric is soon learned: it consists in substituting for the obvious word and thought its diametrical opposite. He praises wild mountains and forests for their domestic air; snow and ice for their warmth . . ." Channing assured Emerson that a new essay of Thoreau's was good. Emerson found that it made him nervous and wretched to read it.

Thoreau had spent only a year on Staten Island. He had not been able to take advantage of the journalistic contacts that Emerson had helped him make in New York. The man of Concord had not been happy away from his woods and fields. When Thoreau decided to build his one-room house on Walden Pond and live what in *Walden* he made the most celebrated episode of his life, Emerson gladly lent him the land, as Alcott, less willingly, lent Thoreau his ax, but Emerson disapproved of the venture. He thought that the first steps to the woods were very enticing but that the end would be want and madness.

When during his second summer at Walden Pond Thoreau was arrested for refusing to pay his poll tax to a government which supported slavery, and was jailed overnight, Emerson was not impressed. He thought the action trivial and meaningless.

Emerson made every effort to get Thoreau's first book, *A Week on the Concord and Merrimack Rivers,* published, then to see that it was properly reviewed and publicized. After Thoreau's return from Walden, he made him a member of his household for another year, but he was often annoyed with him. Thoreau's stubbornness and unnecessary pugnacity in argument grew tiresome. Henry, Emerson said, was always manly and wise but rarely sweet. In the privacy of his study Emerson wrote in 1856: "If I knew only Thoreau, I should think coöperation of good men impossible. Must we always talk for victory, and never once for truth, for comfort, and joy? . . . Always some weary captious paradox to fight you with, and the time and temper wasted."

Elizabeth Hoar said that she loved Henry Thoreau but could not like him. Emerson knew what she meant.

Either Emerson regarded Ellery Channing's verse highly or he wanted to encourage the poet and pettish dilettante, for he used much of it in *The Dial*. Ellery was a gay companion. Emerson strolled often with the whimsical, talkative, quick-changing versifier. It would not have pleased Channing had he known that Emerson noted, "Ellery has the manners and address of a merchant."

It would have pleased Channing even less could he have read a comment in one of Emerson's many long letters to Margaret Fuller, this one dated August 29, 1847. Channing and his family, he wrote her, were off somewhere and, of course, the restless one never wrote when he was away. "His little book on Rome is a pretty good success, is more readable than any thing he has published, and finds some readers & praisers. This perseverance of his in writing & printing, read they or read they not, is an unexpected indemnity which Nature seems to have added to our poet for some small discontinuity which she suffered to occur somewhere in those fine wires."

In one of the moments of clear self-knowledge that men get, Emerson realized that he liked man, but not men. He liked all men but, when he came to know them well, he disliked something about most individuals. He wrote down this very human discovery.

114

Even as he wrote it, he must have known that he was not being completely accurate. The Concord group were his friends and companions. He felt toward them the affection and even the obligations that men feel for those they try to help. Yet he must have realized too, as many of them did, that they were not his equals.

He was their superior in intellect and talent, more gifted, larger, almost different in kind. Emerson was a cosmopolitan who from choice and the accident of his birth and heritage lived in a small New England village. He was by nature and experience the equal of the larger men he had met in Europe.

Carlyle, Wordsworth, and Coleridge had met and talked with him as their equal. He had recognized them and his kinship with them. Even before the appearance of his books, they had recognized the genius in him. In reality, Emerson was of the world of Montaigne and Plutarch, the two writers whom he most admired and to whom he felt closest. He was not only of the Concord world of Alcott and Channing. Perhaps it was this that often led him to feel like a recluse in the village where, besides the solitude he needed, he had plenty of companionship.

Even Thoreau, who was vocal in his insistence upon it, could not achieve Emerson's simplicity. Emerson was at home in Concord's Social Circle. He knew that "A man must have aunts and cousins, must buy carrots and turnips, must have barn and woodshed, must go to market and to the blacksmith's shop, must saunter and sleep and be inferior and silly." Life could not always be, as Alcott tried to make it, moonshine and moonbeams and moon dreams. Life has body in it as well as soul. It cannot all be anaemic straining after ethereal gnats.

Emerson liked farmers and tailors, horse traders and chemists. He preferred them to many of the reformers, scholars, and writers who knocked at his door and invaded the privacy of his square study with its round table and

115

the rocking chair in which he sat and wrote on an atlas balanced across his knees. He shared with the hard-swearing men who drove their sheep and cattle along the roads to market a simplicity that they shared, in a way, with Shakespeare and Montaigne. They took life as it was and lived it. They did not try to turn it into something it was not or to drown it in words or distort it with attempts at ridiculous reforms.

Emerson was beginning to feel the need of excitement again. He needed a taste of the larger world to which, through elements in his temperament as strong as those which bound him to Concord, he belonged. He needed, as he sometimes said, to be "set aglow." He had long wished for a professorship, believing it would keep him active and alert in the scholarly world he knew and liked. For the same reason, he sometimes thought he would like to be a minister again. "Much as I hate the Church," he wrote in his journal in April 1847, "I have wished the pulpit that I might have the stimulus of a stated task." Neither professorship nor pulpit materialized, but something better did.

He had already been invited to give a series of lectures in the cities of Manchester and Birmingham in the industrial north of England. Carlyle urged him to accept, promising that he would see that he was also heard in London. At first Emerson demurred, but he realized that this might prove just the stimulus he needed after his years of hard and demanding work on *The Dial* and concentration on the preparation of his lectures and his books.

On October 5, 1847, he sailed from Boston for Liverpool in the *Washington Irving*. To his surprise, for he disliked the sea, it proved a fast and pleasant voyage. There was a good wind and pleasant weather. There were nine children among the twenty-odd passengers, and not one of them was ill. Even a young stowaway who had run away from home to be a sailor worked happily about the decks.

116

When Emerson landed in Liverpool on October 22, he found a pleasant letter awaiting him from Carlyle. First reporting in Manchester to those who had arranged for his lectures there, Emerson complied with Carlyle's pressing invitation and went immediately to Chelsea, the London borough where the Carlyles now lived. He found the man he had so admired fourteen years earlier unchanged. Assertive, loud-laughing, charged with vigor, Carlyle was trotted out now as a big gun wherever he went. He delighted to disconcert the timid with his devastating remarks. As once before, the two men walked and talked to their mutual content. Besides being a practical Scot, Carlyle was a scholar, widely read and accomplished. He said the same things year after year. It amused Emerson to hear the voluble Carlyle talk against talking, even, prolific writer as he was, rant against writing, but these inconsistencies were no matter. Emerson's admiration was unabated. If anything, his esteem for this lover of truths and hater of shams increased.

The gentle Emerson stood in sharp contrast to the fiery host with whom he stayed for several days, but Emerson was a big gun now too. He was a famed thinker, speaker, and essayist. He was a poet whose *Poems* had appeared earlier this same year. Enthusiastic audiences greeted him when he began his course of lectures. Some of his opinions still shocked the orthodox, but they delighted the liberal and enthralled the young.

His middle- and working-class listeners in Manchester and Birmingham reacted like audiences in Boston or Worcester to the serene presence, the clear blue eyes and resonant voice, the seemingly unconscious skill of the speaker. Emerson spoke in Edinburgh and Glasgow in Scotland. He talked again with Wordsworth, now England's Poet Laureate. He spent two days with Harriet Martineau, the English authoress whose unfavorable report after a brief visit to Alcott's Boston school had helped cause its failure. He spent several days at Oxford, where in the

117

Bodleian Library he saw the manuscript of Plato, who had so greatly influenced his thought.

As he did when he lectured in the United States, Emerson stayed in inns at first. Soon he was the welcome and appreciative guest at home after English home. In Edinburgh, Thomas De Quincey, author of the *Confessions of an English Opium-Eater,* now a gentle, elderly man, walked ten miles through the rain to dine with him on a Sunday. Emerson's letters and journal were charged with a new vigor. Though he made the usual modest disclaimers, he reveled in the people he met, in the attentions he received, and in this new opportunity to scrutinize England and the English. He crammed his notebooks with the close observations and shrewd comments he was to turn into *English Traits,* 1856, perhaps the most coherent of all Emerson's books and still fresh and pleasantly readable.

Emerson met and liked Alfred Lord Tennyson, England's most popular poet. He had about him an air of general superiority which Emerson said he found most satisfactory. "He is tall, scholastic-looking, no dandy, but a great deal of plain strength about him . . . ; quiet, sluggish sense and strength, refined, as the English are, and good-humoured. . . . Take away Hawthorne's bashfulness, and let him talk easily and fast, and you would have a pretty good Tennyson."

When his series of lectures in the English Midlands was over, Emerson decided to visit Paris. Friends suggested that Tennyson go with him. Tennyson said he would if Emerson would go to Italy instead. Emerson was tempted, but there would not be time enough if he was to return in time for his London engagements. In the end he went to France alone, Tennyson pretending to feel certain he would never get back alive because of the revolution in France that year. Emerson spent three pleasant weeks in Paris.

Back in London, he saw much of Carlyle again and through Carlyle, many of his friends who already knew

Emerson through his books. The historian and scholar George Bancroft, who had graduated from Harvard College the year Emerson entered, was now American ambassador to Great Britain. He opened the doors of the embassy and the doors of many of the great and famous in England for Emerson.

He met scientists and actresses, writers and artists, noblemen and commoners. He attended a Free-Trade banquet where both Richard Cobden and John Bright spoke. Through the good offices of his influential friends, he was made a temporary member of the Athenaeum, a famed London club of literary, artistic, and scientific men. Emerson prized this privilege not only because only ten foreigners were eligible for the Athenaeum at any one time, but also because it gave him a London home. He could sit in the Athenaeum and write his letters, dine there, and, if he wished, eat in the coffee-room at cost. Richard Monckton Milnes, poet and politician; Henry Hart Milman, Dean of St. Paul's Cathedral; Henry Crabb Robinson, one of the founders of University College; and "other good men," as Emerson called them, were usually to be found at the Athenaeum. It was largely through Milnes, who was also Baron Houghton, that Emerson came to mingle in London society.

As Carlyle had promised, Emerson spoke before England's aristocracy. One of his lectures was on "Natural Aristocracy." In it, he made few concessions to his ruling-class audience. He spoke of the duties and obligations of the favored classes, and in one passage described the idle and perfumed gentleman. Such men, he said, served no one. They lived on the labor of others. They ate their bread, but after breakfast could not remember that those who had provided it were human beings. One titled listener, somewhat affronted, suggested that Emerson omit the passage the next time he gave the lecture. No one else who attended

119

any of the six lectures Emerson gave in London objected to it.

Emerson dined one evening with the novelist William Makepeace Thackeray, and with Lord Auckland, Lady Castlereagh, and the Bishop of Oxford. He dined on other occasions with Lord Morpeth, Lady Harriet Baring, and Lady Ashburton. He was entertained by the Prime Minister and his lady, Lord and Lady Palmerston. At the Marquis of Northampton's he saw Prince Albert, consort of Queen Victoria.

All of these names and more Emerson carefully noted in his journal, and, humanly pleased at the attention he was receiving, reported in his letters home. Lord Lovelace had called on him. He had met Lady Byron and visited the poet Leigh Hunt. In one happy letter he told Elizabeth Hoar that he had lunched with the Duchess of Sutherland, explaining that Sutherland House was "the best in the kingdom, the Queen's not excepted." The Duchess had made much of him, and he had met the Duke of Argyle.

Emerson saw Dickens, Disraeli, Lockhart (critic and son-in-law of Sir Walter Scott), Cruikshank (cartoonist and illustrator of Dickens's work), Jenny Lind, the Duke of Wellington. Whom of the rich and famous did he not meet? Carlyle, Tennyson, Coleridge, Wordsworth, and Macaulay, he decided, could not be matched in America, certainly not in Concord—not even in Cambridge.

London seemed to Emerson the capital of the world, a place where men had lived since there were men. He walked its streets, watching the faces of the people. He wandered the sprawling city until he reached the straggle of houses at each end and then the suburbs.

On Friday, July 7, Emerson went on a jaunt with Carlyle. They took a train through Hampshire to Salisbury, then, Carlyle talking all the time, went by carriage to Amesbury where they stopped at the George Inn. After dinner they walked to Salisbury Plain to view Stonehenge,

120

Emerson and Thomas Carlyle were at Stonehenge in July 1848.

121

the great prehistoric stone circle about one hundred feet in diameter. They clambered around and over the stones brought there by ancient peoples until Carlyle found a sheltered nook where he could light his cigar. Emerson was awed by the ancient outdoor temple, and even Carlyle was impressed enough to grow subdued.

After a half hour of exploring, they went by dogcart over the Downs to visit Wilton Hall, seat of the Earls of Pembroke. Carlyle had obtained a letter of introduction from its owner, Sidney Herbert, to his housekeeper, so they were shown over the stately home and grounds.

On their return journey they inspected Salisbury Cathedral and spent a rainy Sunday at Bishops Waltham, Emerson trying to answer their host's questions about America and its future. They saw Winchester and its cathedral, where King Alfred was crowned and was buried. From Winchester the two men returned to London.

Before he left England, Emerson went with other friends to visit Stokes Poges in Buckinghamshire, scene of Thomas Gray's "Elegy Written in a Country Churchyard." He saw Queen Victoria's apartment in Windsor Castle, and at Eton College "six or seven hundred boys, the flower of English youth."

Emerson was a full man again when he sailed for home July 15, 1848. He had the material for *Representative Men* in the lectures he had given in England. He had the material for *English Traits* in his journal.

This time the sea lived up to his worst expectations. "The road from Liverpool to New York is long, crooked, rough, rainy, and windy. Even good company will hardly make it agreeable. Four meals a day is the usual expedient, four and five (and the extreme remedy shows the exasperation of the case), and much wine and porter are the amusements of wise men in this sad place."

8

Emerson had been glad to be away. Now he was glad to be home. Reinvigorated, he began immediately to prepare his English lectures for publication in book form, and to ready the series of lectures which, as usual, he gave in the winter of 1849. He was busy with his writing in the morning, with his walks and talks in the afternoon, and happy renewing his home life.

Ellen and Edith were growing up. Edward Waldo, the Emersons' fourth and last child, was five years old. For his children Emerson wished both the cultural advantages of the city and the peace and beauty of the country. He had found that he needed both.

He walked with them and skated with them when the ice was firm. An old pair of skates always hung in his study closet. He showed an interest in everything that the two girls and his small son did. He wanted to know about their work and their play, about their interests and their companions.

Even on holidays he encouraged them first to work at their tasks, then to play. If a quarrel broke out, he would send one of the combatants outside to see whether or not it was raining or another into the kitchen to make sure the stove was still lighted. Remembering his own boyhood days as a stranger in the Concord school, he urged them to be pleasant to any new boy or girl.

When one of his daughters told him that a new student had appeared that day, he asked if she had spoken to her. She admitted she had not and defended herself by saying she could think of nothing to say. Next time, her father told her, if she could think of nothing else, she could ask the newcomer to admire her shoestrings.

For a time the four Alcott girls, the three Emerson children, and a few others went to school in Emerson's barn. When school was over for the day, Emerson sometimes piled them all into a hay cart and took them berry picking in season or picnicking or bathing in Walden Pond. He showed them patches of hidden wildflowers he had discovered in the woods or told them of the birds and small animals and their haunts as Thoreau had showed him.

Although he could not be informal even with close friends, to most of whom he was always "Mr. Emerson," he was at ease in the intimacy of his family. When it was a new fad, he tried taking a cold bath in the morning, came shivering down to breakfast, and announced that he thought the composition of cold water must be one part hydrogen and three parts conceit. The cold baths and sleeping with the windows open were just new forms of self-righteousness, he decided, and he gave them both up.

He called Lidian "Queenie," sometimes, facetiously, "Wifey." He sometimes amazed his children—for they had never known him as a minister—by spouting Scripture, often twisting the exact words of the King James version for humorous effect.

Once when one of the importunate who were always knocking at the door of the big square house came to demand attention and support, Emerson told his family in a tone of affected surprise that the man looked more like a gentleman than a philosopher, implying that most of his scholarly friends looked otherwise.

Emerson advised his children to finish each day and be done with it. Probably they had made some mistakes. Forget them, he suggested, and begin the new day afresh. He tried to show them how practical things should be done, but he did not always succeed. One day he and Edward were diving about trying to drive a calf into the barn. An Irish maid could stand their clumsiness no longer. She put her finger into the calf's mouth and led it quietly into the barn.

The children were a joy, but there were other people he could do without. He was courteous to the stream of visitors who, as Hawthorne noted, continually descended on him. Some he welcomed. The crackpots and the uncouth he heard quietly and sent on their way as gently as he could, but he was not always able to rid himself of some unwanted guest.

It was always, he noted, the imperfect people, the half-educated, the thinkers of half-thoughts, who besieged him. He could always tell when people did not want him. Why could not some of these see that he did not want them and was only being civil because he had to? Emerson decided unhappily that he could count on his fingers all the sane men that ever came to him.

Emerson had seen Europe again and reveled in it. Now he set his face toward a new country, the American West. In 1850 he went to Kentucky, where he explored Mammoth Cave, then sailed down the Ohio and up the Mississippi to St. Louis. He crossed Illinois by stage, Michigan by railroad, and returned to Concord by way of Niagara Falls. This was the first of the lecturing trips westward that Emerson was to continue making for the next twenty years.

Each year Emerson spent at least two winter months in travel from Maine to the country west of the Mississippi, and most of the time there were few of the civilized amenities he had known in England and knew in Concord. While he was away he spoke every night except Sundays and spent the time between lectures struggling from one place to the next. He traveled in dirty and airless railroad cars, in horse-drawn coaches, even in open sleighs. He got stuck in the mud. He got stuck in the snow. He got soaked in torrential rains. He slept in cold spare bedrooms, in wretched taverns, or in resplendent hotels.

Emerson liked the merchants and traveling salesmen he met in the trains, saying they were more manly and had better manners than most of the scholars he knew. He liked most of the hotels, but he said that the air seemed buttered and often the whole place was like a ventilated beefsteak.

Several times he crossed the Mississippi in an open boat, partly in water, partly on ice. By 1855, he said, he had crossed it three times on foot. He wrote Lidian, William, sometimes his mother, who lived in the room above his study until her death in 1854, of his varied adventures. Often the letters to Lidian contained checks—in one he told her how to endorse them—or small sums of money which he had earned in places where it amused him to see himself advertised sometimes as a poet and essayist, sometimes as "the celebrated metaphysician."

On March 21, 1851, he wrote his wife that he had reached Pittsburgh after a long journey from Philadelphia by rail and canal boat. He had had little food and less sleep. Two nights he had spent on the train. A third he had endured on the floor of the boat "where the cushion allowed me for a bed was crossed at the knees by another tier of sleepers as long-limbed as I,—so that in the air was a wreath of legs." He got some sleep, he admitted, for he had been tired enough to sleep standing.

In January 1853 he was in Springfield, Illinois. "It rains and thaws incessantly," he wrote Lidian, "and, if we step

126

Emerson traveled the West when the West was new.

off the short street we go up to the shoulders, perhaps, in mud. My chamber is a cabin; my fellow boarders are legislators. . . . Two or three ex-governors live in the house."

There was plenty of raw, cold country for Emerson on these lecture tours; plenty of arriving at country inns at four o'clock in the morning and getting the worst bed in the house. Once he traveled all day through Wisconsin behind a team of horses. For long distances there was no water for either passengers or animals. People along the route had only melted snow for their household water needs.

When they reached one inn after crossing the Mississippi in a skiff, the landlord and his clerks had to rub the numbed hands of the travelers and thaw them out before a good fire before they could feed and bed them. Emerson must often have wistfully remembered the Athenaeum Club, Sutherland House, and the other comfortable homes he had known in England as well as his own snug study in Concord.

Often he wished he were home, but business was bad in some of these years. Dividends on his investments were cut down or not paid at all. Lecturing then became his chief source of income. His books brought him in little, for he had made poor bargains with his publishers. Sometimes when he was tired, Emerson grew disgusted with his lecturing and compared it to puppet shows and other vaudeville entertainment. He knew better. His lecturing may have been, as he called it, an economic expedient, but it was also his chief means of expression, the release of his natural talent. He would have been less than himself without it.

After years of his extensive and complicated winter lecture schedules, he found himself unable to resist a lucrative offer to appear in Chicago. He compared the bargain to a wager. " 'I'll bet you fifty dollars a day that you will not leave your library, and wade and ride and run and suffer all manner of indignities and stand up for an hour each night reading in a hall'; and I answered, 'I'll bet I will.' I do it and win the $900."

Emerson had opened the first series of biographical lectures he ever gave, in Boston in 1834, with an introductory lecture on the tests of great men. It was of the heroes of the ages that he spoke again in Boston in 1845 and 1846, then in England in 1847 and 1848.

Emerson thought it was natural to believe in great men. Men had always believed in them. The gods of fable had been such men. He liked them. "I admire great men of all classes," he said in the introductory chapter of *Representative Men,* which was published in 1850, "those who stand for facts, and for thoughts; I like rough and smooth, 'Scourges of God,' and 'Darlings of the human race.' . . . I applaud a sufficient man, an officer equal to his office; captains, ministers, senators. I like a master standing firm on legs of iron, well-born, rich, handsome, eloquent, loaded with advantages, drawing all men by fascination . . ."

In "Self-Reliance" Emerson had defined what for him was the truly great man. It was "he who in the midst of the crowd keeps with perfect sweetness the independence of solitude." The truly great man, he made clear once more in *Representative Men,* is the man who is himself. He is true to that in him which partakes of the nature of all men. He works. He expresses this basic nature, and his example makes other men aware of the greatness within themselves.

In this book Emerson wrote of six men who represented different activities and different kinds of greatness. They were: Plato, or the philosopher; Swedenborg, or the mystic; Montaigne, or the skeptic; Shakespeare, or the poet; Napoleon, or the man of the world; Goethe, or the writer.

Napoleon was strong by insight. He depended upon himself. He asked no one's advice. Napoleon understood his business, something which Emerson always approved. Napoleon was direct. "He would shorten a straight line to come at his object." Napoleon had prudence, good sense, and the will to achieve.

Emerson made his admiration of Napoleon clear. Then he gave his judgment: "He was thoroughly unscrupulous. He would steal, slander, assassinate, drown and poison, as his interest dictated. He had no generosity, but mere vulgar hatred; he was intensely selfish; he was perfidious; he cheated at cards; he was a prodigious gossip, and opened letters . . . It does not appear that he listened at keyholes, or at least that he was caught at it."

Napoleon was self-reliant, and he expressed his own nature that was part of the nature of all men; but his egotism and his actions were deadly to other men. His aims were selfish. Emerson dismissed him as an imposter and a rogue who left the world worse than he found it.

For Emerson, the greatest of great men was Plato, the Greek thinker and writer who lived 427–347 B.C. Emerson owed more of his basic thought to Plato than to any other writer. Emerson's idealism—the belief that material things have their real existence in the spiritual idea behind them—was Plato's. Plato's reiterated advice was "Know thyself." Emerson urged people to know themselves but to go a step farther, to act on this knowledge, to trust themselves.

Both Plato and his teacher, Socrates, believed that it was virtuous for a man to act in accordance with his true nature developed through inborn knowledge of the good. So did Emerson. Long before Emerson, Plato and Socrates had believed in intuition, that is, that man has direct and immediate knowledge of unseen spiritual realities.

Plato, Emerson said in *Representative Men,* had been the Bible of the learned for 2,200 years. From him had come the ideas that were still discussed and written about. Plato had taken all the arts and sciences, all knowledge, as his province. "Plato is philosophy, and philosophy, Plato." Plato had "almost impressed language and the primary forms of thought with his name and seal." Plato took all that was known in his own time, and the thoughts he wished from men who had lived and written before him, and made them his own. He was the full man. He was himself and by being himself partook of the nature of all men. "He is a great average man; one who, to the best thinking, adds a proportion and equality in his faculties, so that men see in him their own dreams . . ."

Emerson had first read Montaigne's *Essais,* in an English translation by Charles Cotton, when he was twenty-one years old. When he was twenty-nine, he wrote in his journal that the book so accurately and sincerely described his own thoughts and feelings that he felt as if he might have written it in some former life. No book before or since ever meant so much to him.

Emerson mentions the *Essais* of the sixteenth-century French writer again and again in his journal, and always with enthusiasm. Montaigne was robust, generous, and downright. "With all my heart I embrace the grand old sloven," Emerson wrote when he was in his thirties. He found Montaigne's essays "full of fun, poetry, business, divinity, philosophy, anecdote, smut." They dealt, Emerson wrote, in marrow, corn-barn, and flour barrel, in wife, friends, and valet. Reading Montaigne always inspirited Emerson. Montaigne was eminently sane, and all the sanity and common sense in Emerson responded to him.

In *Representative Men* Emerson uses the same words to describe his discovery of Montaigne that he had used in his journal years before. He speaks with the same enthusiasm. Montaigne was a skeptic. He did not pretend to be certain of anything. Emerson saw nothing amiss in a wise skepticism—knowledge is knowing that we cannot know—and Montaigne was as wise as he was skeptical. There was salt and sinew in his sentences. Montaigne was honestly himself. He was all men when they are fully alive and walking a middle path between extremes of belief in some favorite and probably erroneous idea and no idea at all.

Shakespeare owned a copy of Montaigne's *Essais* in an English translation. It was the only book known certainly to have been in his library. Ben Jonson owned a copy. Lord Byron read Montaigne with satisfaction. Emerson's biography of the intellectually curious, liberal-minded, tolerant, and frank Montaigne rings with his approval of the man.

A real poet is in accord with his own heart and with his own times. He reflects both his inner self and life around him. Shakespeare was and did. Inconceivably wise, he was "a full man who liked to talk." Shakespeare took the material for his plays and poems wherever he found it. He took from life, from books, from other writers, but what he took he made his own through the originality of his expression. Emerson did the same thing, but he was speaking of Shakespeare when he wrote, "He steals by this apology,—that what he takes has no worth where he finds it and the greatest where he leaves it."

The secret of Shakespeare's poetry, Emerson wrote, was that merely reading for sense brought out the music of the rhyme and rhythm. Emerson knew that in all good writing, sense and sound cannot successfully be separated.

Though Carlyle worshipped the German romantic poet, dramatist, novelist, scientist, and scholar, Emerson did not have the same natural affinity for Johann Wolfgang Goethe that he had for Plato and Shakespeare. Goethe, he admitted, had written some of the best things about nature that were ever penned, but Emerson could not place this "amateur of all the arts" with those writers, like Plato, Montaigne, and Shakespeare, who meant most to him. Yet Goethe, he said, was the soul of his century just as Napoleon had been the representative of its popular external life.

What Emerson wrote of Goethe in this essay is of less

132

interest now than what he wrote about the writer, which he had chosen Goethe to exemplify. Emerson might as well have been writing of Carlyle, Coleridge, Thoreau, himself, or any other natural and serious writer.

> Men are born to write. The gardener saves every slip and seed and peach-stone: his vocation is to be a planter of plants. Not less does the writer attend his affair. Whatever he beholds or experiences, comes to him as a model and sits for its picture. He counts it all nonsense that they say, that some things are undescribable. He believes that all that can be thought can be written, first or last; and he would report the Holy Ghost, or attempt it. Nothing so broad, so subtle, or so dear, but comes therefore commended to his pen, and he will write. In his eyes, a man is the faculty of reporting, and the universe is the possibility of being reported. In conversation, in calamity, he finds new materials; as our German poet said, "Some god gave me the power to paint what I suffer." He draws his rents from rage and pain. By acting rashly, he buys the power of talking wisely. Vexations and a tempest of passion only fill his sail . . .

Certainly, Emerson in his writings had drawn on the hardships of his boyhood, on the tragic as he knew it through the deaths of his first wife, his brothers, and his small son. Certainly he drew on the idealism of Plato, the optimism of Alcott, the skepticism of Montaigne and Hawthorne, and the damn-your-eyes independence and nature lore of Henry Thoreau. Certainly he reported the universe as he saw it. Perhaps in the highest reaches of his poetry and prose it was an ethereality as subtle and intangible as the Holy Ghost that he strove to capture and report in shining words.

9

There is neither preface nor introduction to this book. Emerson had no use for either one.

Margaret Fuller left New York and the Greeley household for Europe, from which she sent back stories that were published on the front page of the *New York Tribune*. In Italy she became an adherent of the Italian patriot Mazzini, siding with him in the republican revolution of 1848. She married the Marquis Ossoli, and in the spring of 1850 started back to the United States with her husband and their small child. The night before it would have anchored in New York harbor, their ship was wrecked off Fire Island. The body of the drowned child was found. Those of the Marquis and of Margaret Fuller Ossoli were not. Emerson despatched Thoreau to the scene to locate what he could of Margaret's belongings, but Thoreau could find only a carpetbag of Ossoli's, a button from his coat, and a black leather trunk containing some books and papers.

With James Freeman Clarke and William Henry Channing, Emerson undertook to edit a two-volume *Memoir of Margaret Fuller*. When one of them suggested he write a preface to the book, which was published in 1852, Emerson firmly refused.

He wrote Channing, "I hate to hear of swelling the book. . . . Amputate, amputate. And why a preface? If eight pages are there, let them be gloriously blank. No, no preface . . . I do not mean to write a needless syllable."

Emerson did not believe in leading up to a subject. He was not interested in watching a pitcher's awesome windup. He wanted him to throw the ball, the harder the better. He had found fault with Hawthorne's long and unnecessary introductions. When you had something to say, Emerson said, the best thing was to get on with it. He wrote no explanatory openings for his own books but broke squarely into his subjects. The most he would do was preface his essays with short verse passages that said pithily what he said at greater length in the body of the essay.

To Emerson, writing was all-important. He agreed with the writer of Ecclesiastes that there is no new thing under the sun. All the great thoughts have been thought. Anything a man can think has been thought by someone centuries before him. It is the manner of expressing a thought that can be individual and original.

Children, Emerson noted, cry, scream, and stamp their feet because at first that is the only way in which they can express what they feel and try to say what they want. When they learn to talk and can tell what is bothering them or what they need, they grow gentler. Ignorant men and women shout and swear because they have not learned to say accurately what they mean. Young men and women sigh and weep because they do not yet know how to make others understand them. They lack adequate powers of communication.

Men and women love to communicate, and what they think they have to say bothers them until they can say it. There is a universal pleasure in conversation, but some men are born with added powers to speak and write.

Such men, and Emerson numbered himself among them, continually develop their powers of expression. The writer must have inborn talent to start with, he thought, but he must also be a man, a formed and determined individual whose character and insight give life and light to his sentences. Montaigne had been such a man. "The sincerity and marrow of the man reaches to his sentences. . . . It is the language of conversation transferred to a book. Cut these words, and they would bleed; they are vascular and alive. One has the same pleasure in it that he feels in listening to the necessary speech of men about their work. . . . For blacksmiths and teamsters do not trip in their speech; it is a shower of bullets."

Emerson liked his words to strike like a shower of bullets. He hated vague, mumbling, indecisive words. Emerson always preferred the short, hard, Anglo-Saxon words. He seldom said that he disliked or even detested anything. He said he hated it. The word "hate" appears again and again in his journal. He was still a Boston preacher when he wrote, "I hate goodies [do-gooders and the mealy-mouthed]. I hate goodness that preaches." Again he wrote, "I hate quotations. Tell me what you know." Emerson pleaded for direct, hard speech. "Hard clouds, and hard expressions, and hard manners, I love," he wrote in 1843. He used "love" as often as he used "hate." It was the hard and forceful word. It said what he meant.

Emerson made his writing tight and terse. When he was turning his lectures into essays, he cut out every unnecessary word and retained only those essential to his meaning. A writer should omit every dull, slow-moving sentence. "Blot them out and read them again and you will find what words drag. If you use a word for a fraction of its meaning, it must drag. It is like a pebble inserted in a mosaic. Blot out the superlatives, the negatives, the dismals, the adjectives, and *very*. And finally see that you have not omitted the word which the piece was written to state."

Emerson loved Carlyle for what the man was. He approved of Carlyle's ideas because he shared them, but he most admired Carlyle as a writer. Carlyle's greatest contribution, he said, was to the art of writing. Dante, too, knew how to write. Like Byron, Burke, and Carlyle, he threw all his vigor into his work. Dante could say "damn" if he pleased, and sometimes he did please—and that pleased Emerson. Emerson thought that Tennyson had little to say in his poetry but that he said it superbly. His contribution, too, was to the art of writing. Emerson saw Tennyson as a master of the art of versification.

Emerson used as few adjectives, as few "very's," as he could. He seldom underlined. He disapproved of italics. If your writing was sound, the italics would show without being there. He condemned the superlative. In a lecture on the subject he said, "All this overstatement is needless. A little fact is worth a whole limbo of dreams, and I can well spare the exaggerations which appear to me to be screens to conceal ignorance." He wished he could stop people from saying "the best I ever saw" or "I never in my life." They'd probably seen better or as good and their "never" was "hardly ever" or more often than that. Forcible understatement was always preferable to loud overstatement.

When Emerson wrote, he followed his own precepts. He said what he had to say with all the force at his command, said it shortly and sharply, often in striking imagery. Unless he had to, he did not use the language of books. He used the everyday language of men and women about him. His work abounds in examples.

Travelling is a fool's paradise. Our first journeys discover to us the indifference of places. At home I dream that at Naples, at Rome, I can be intoxicated with beauty and lose my sadness. I pack my trunk, embrace my friends, embark on the sea and at last wake up in Naples, and there beside

137

me is the stern fact, the sad self, unrelenting, identical, that I fled from. I seek the Vatican and the palaces. I affect to be intoxicated with sights and suggestions, but I am not intoxicated. My giant goes with me wherever I go.

"Self-Reliance"

For every grain of wit there is a grain of folly. For everything you have missed, you have gained something else; and for everything you gain, you lose something. If riches increase, they are increased that use them. If the gatherer gathers too much, Nature takes out of the man what she puts into his chest; swells the estate, but kills the owner.

"Compensation"

The Normans came out of France into England worse men than they went into it one hundred and sixty years before. . . . Twenty thousand thieves landed at Hastings. These founders of the House of Lords were greedy and ferocious dragoons, sons of greedy and ferocious pirates. They were all alike, they took everything they could carry, they burned, harried, violated, tortured, and killed, until everything English was brought to the verge of ruin. Such however is the illusion of antiquity and wealth, that decent and dignified men now existing boast their descent from these filthy thieves, who showed a far juster conviction of their own merits, by assuming for their types the swine, goat, jackal, leopard, wolf and snake, which they severally resembled.

English Traits

We are students of words; we are shut up in schools and colleges, and recitation-rooms, for ten or fifteen years, and come out at last with a bag of wind, a memory of words, and do not know a thing. We cannot use our hands, or our legs, or our eyes, or our arms. We do not know an edible root in the woods, we cannot tell our course by the stars, nor the hour of the day by the sun. It is well if we can swim and skate. We are afraid of a horse, of a cow, of a dog, of a snake, of a spider. The Roman rule was to teach a boy

138

nothing that he could not learn standing. The old English rule was, "All summer in the field, and all winter in the study."

"New England Reformers"

The ancient Greeks called the world . . . beauty. Such is the constitution of all things, or such the plastic power of the human eye, that the primary forms, as the sky, the mountains, the tree, the animal, give us a delight *in and for themselves;* a pleasure arising from outline, color, motion, and grouping. This seems partly owing to the eye itself. The eye is the best of artists. By the mutual action of its structure and of the laws of light, perspective is produced, which integrates every mass of objects, of what character soever, into a well colored and shaded globe, so that where the particular objects are mean and unaffecting, the landscape which they compose is round and symmetrical.

Nature

The utmost that can be demanded of the gentleman is that he be incapable of a lie. There is a man who has good sense, is well informed, well read, obliging, cultivated, capable, and has an absolute devotion to the truth. He always means what he says, and says what he means, however courteously. You may spit upon him;—nothing could induce him to spit upon you,—no praises, and no possessions, no compulsion of public opinion. You may kick him;—he will think it the kick of a brute: but he is not a brute and will not kick you in return. But neither your knife and pistol, nor your gifts and courting will ever make the smallest impression on his vote or word; for he is truth's man, and will speak and act the truth until he dies.

Journal, December 14, 1850

You cannot refine Mr. Lincoln's taste, extend his horizon, or clear his judgment; he will not walk dignifiedly through the traditional part of the President of America, but will pop out his head at each railroad station and make a little speech, and get into an argument with Squire A. and Judge B. . . .

But this we must be ready for, and let the clown appear, and hug ourselves that we are well off, if we have got good nature, honest meaning, and fidelity to public interest, with bad manners,—instead of an elegant *roué* and malignant self-seeker.

Journal, October 9, 1863

Alas for America, as I must so often say, the ungirt, the diffuse, the profuse, procumbent,—one wide ground juniper, out of which no cedar, no oak will rear up a mast to the clouds! It all runs to leaves, to suckers, to tendrils, to miscellany. The air is loaded with poppy, with imbecility, with dispersion and sloth.

Eager, solicitous, hungry, rabid, busy-bodied America attempting many things, vain, ambitious to feel thy own existence, and convince others of thy talent, by attempting and hastily accomplishing much; yes, catch thy breath and correct thyself, and failing here, prosper out there; speed and fever are never greatness; but reliance and serenity and waiting.

America is formless, has no terrible and beautiful condensation.

Journal, June 1847

In 1865, Emerson was invited by a group of students to lecture at Williams College in the northwest corner of Massachusetts. He went to give one lecture, but he was so enthusiastically received that he remained a week. One of the students, Charles J. Woodbury, appointed himself to look after Emerson and spent the greater part of the week walking and talking with him and arranging for him to give additional lectures in the nearby cities of Pittsfield and North Adams. They talked much about writing and Emerson told the young man of twenty-two many of the thoughts he had already recorded in his journal. A quarter-century later Woodbury reported some of these comments about writing in his *Talks with Ralph Waldo Emerson.*

"Say it! Out with it! Don't lead up to it! Don't try to let your hearer down from it. That is to be commonplace. Say it with all the grace and force you can, and stop . . ." Emerson urged his own plan of starting with no plan or skeleton. The natural one would develop as you wrote. Then "knock away all scaffolding."

When he wished, Emerson could write a book on a simple and straightforward plan. He wrote such a book in *English Traits*. He preferred, for very different content, the almost patternless form of his essays. Here he depended not on architectural construction but on the force and brilliance, the ringing tone, with which he uttered his intuitive convictions. He spoke or wrote in simple, striking words, sentences, even paragraphs. Then he expressed the same thoughts again in different words and figures of speech, until his essays seem not bounded wholes but heapings-up of multicolored brilliance. His sentences and images stir and dazzle the reader with the beauty which Emerson felt and imbue him with the truths of which he was convinced. At the same time they convey something of Emerson's own lucid wisdom.

Like most thoughtful writers, Emerson preferred poetry to prose. He was wise enough to know and say that the whole secret of poetry can never be explained, but he defined the poet as a liberating god, one whose vision frees men from the commonplaces of life and gives them an insight into the beauty of the universe and lets them hear a music that, but for the poet, ordinarily goes unheard.

Emerson did not consider a poem a matter of rhyme and meter alone. To him a poem was "a thought so passionate and alive that, like the spirit of a plant or animal, it has an architecture of its own and adorns nature with a new thing."

Emerson valued his poems more than he valued his prose. He felt that poetry was the highest form of expression of which he was capable, and he knew that he could attain it only in his best moments. He could work at an essay or a lecture. He could not sit down and deliberately write a poem. When they met on a Boston street one day, he told the Reverend William Alger, "I can breathe at any time, but I can only whistle when the right pucker comes."

Once when James Freeman Clarke wrote asking him for some of his poems to publish in *The Western Messenger*, Emerson sent him two that he had written previously, one of them sixteen years before. He wished he had newer verses to send, but he had not. "It seems strange," he wrote Clarke in his accompanying letter, "seeing the delight we take in verses, that we can so seldom write them, and so are not ashamed to lay up old ones . . . instead of improvising them as freely as the wind blows."

Though many of his poems had appeared in *The Dial* and other publications, Emerson did not publish a volume of his poetry until 1846, and then only after his publishers had been asking for three years. His *Poems* contained many of his best, and their value was immediately recognized. Though the book was dated 1847, it was published in time for sale at Christmas 1846. On January 9, 1847, the *New York Tribune* reprinted "Wood-Notes," "The Apology," "Musketaquid," "The Snow Storm," "Monadnoc," and "The Day's Ration" on the front page. The newspaper did not attempt to review the book. A note following the reprinted verses simply said, "He who can read the volume now before us and not feel its author is in a high and pure sense a poet, is not likely to be persuaded by anything else we could offer."

Emerson used the simplest rhythms in his verse because he felt them to be the most natural. Often when he was walking he would hum these rhythms—lines of eight or ten syllables with the accent falling on every second syllable—to himself as he moved along. He thought these rhythms came from the beat of the pulse, the beat of the heart. Thus they were universal, felt by men and women everywhere.

The subjects of his poems were the subjects he wrote about in his prose. His poems were about nature as he saw and loved it, and about man and his relation to his universe. Few of Emerson's poems are musical. Most are poems of ideas which he expressed in concentrated, compact, and clear-edged lines. They are more thoughtful than emotional. Sometimes, though, they seem deeply felt. Often they have a sharpness, a sting in them; often a touch of humor.

Humor touches the thought in "The Humble-Bee."

Burly, dozing humble-bee,
Where thou art is clime for me.
Let them sail for Porto Rique,
Far-off heat through seas to seek;
I will follow thee alone,
Thou animated torrid-zone!
Zigzag steerer, desert cheerer,
Let me chase thy waving lines;
Keep me nearer, me thy hearer,
Singing over shrubs and vines. . . .
Wiser far than human seer,
Yellow-breeched philosopher!
Seeing only what is fair,
Sipping only what is sweet,
Thou dost mock at fate and care,
Leave the chaff and take the wheat.
When the fierce northwestern blast
Cools sea and land so far and fast,
Thou already slumberest deep;
Woe and want thou canst outsleep;
Want and woe, which torture us,
Thy sleep makes ridiculous.

The last poem in Emerson's 1846 volume was the familiar "Concord Hymn." Next to last was his long "Threnody." This was Emerson's poetic lament for Waldo, a father's outcry for his lost son. It is a moving poem which has been compared to Milton's "Lycidas" and to Shelley's "Adonais." It is a deeply personal poem in which Emerson calls Waldo "a wondrous child"—"the most beautiful and sweet of human youth"—"nature's sweet marvel"—"the hyacinthine boy."

Emerson describes Waldo in his wicker baby carriage soberly watching the parade of children past their fence and gate on the way to school. As the boy grew a little older, men and women passing forgot their errands and stopped to share his games. On the morning of Waldo's death, the cocks crowed and the snowbirds chirped as they always did. Other life remained, but not Waldo's. No angel had stopped to save the child whose genius, Emerson felt, promised so much for the world.

> The South-wind brings
> Life, sunshine and desire,
> And on every mount and meadow
> Breathes aromatic fire;
> But over the dead he has no power,
> The lost, the lost, he cannot restore;
> And, looking over the hills, I mourn
> The darling who shall not return. . . .
>
> The painted sled stands where it stood;
> The kennel by the corded wood;
> His gathered sticks to stanch the wall
> Of the snow-tower, when snow should fall;
> The ominous hole he dug in the sand,
> And childhood's castles built or planned;
> His daily haunts I well discern,—
> The poultry-yard, the shed, the barn,—
> And every inch of garden ground
> Paced by the blessed feet around,
> From the roadside to the brook
> Whereinto he loved to look.
> Step the meek fowls where erst they ranged;

The wintry garden lies unchanged;
The brook into the stream runs on;
But the deep-eyed boy is gone. . . .

The eager fate which carried thee
Took the largest part of me:
For this losing is true dying;
This is lordly man's down-lying. . . .

"Threnody" is an outcry of pain. It has little artifice. It is lament, but it has its own restraint and dignity in grief. It is simple. It touches the heart with its mention of the simple objects fraught with emotion for the poet.

As characteristic of Emerson's poetry is the far different "Compensation," a poem which he prefixed to his essay on the subject. This is intellectual poetry which depends for its poetic quality on the nobility of the thought and the grandeur of the image. Emerson used the language of physics and astronomy and joined these to his idea of the eternal balance in nature and in human nature. The starkness of the poem makes it sound like the modern verse of a century and more after he wrote it.

The wings of Time are black and white,
Pied with morning and with night.
Mountain tall and ocean deep
Trembling balance duly keep.
In changing moon, in tidal wave,
Glows the feud of Want and Have.
Gauge of more and less through space
Electric star and pencil plays.
The lonely Earth amid the balls
That hurry through the eternal halls,
A makeweight flying to the void,
Supplemental asteroid,
Or compensatory spark,
Shoots across the neutral Dark.

Emerson was a poet in his unceasing endeavor to penetrate appearances and reach through to, then express, the spirit of a thing. With Plato, he believed that all great thoughts come not from the mind but from the heart.

He never quite got over the ambition he had had when he graduated from Harvard to become a teacher of speaking and writing. More than once in successful mid-career he commented wonderingly and with evident disappointment that not even the poorest country college ever offered him a professorship of rhetoric. He felt he could have taught his subject well.

Certainly he was an exquisite literary craftsman, fully conscious of both the difficulties and the possibilities in writing. He wrote with all the skill he had, then rewrote with all the intelligence he could bring to bear as a critic. He worked with meticulous care on his writing, especially on his prose writing, to which he often gave more essentially poetic meaning than he could express in some of his poems that he wrote with comparatively less care and craftsmanship.

It is probable that Emerson would have taught writing well and could have instilled in his students something of his own appreciation of writing and shared some of his external skills with them. He could not have made them Emersons. As he wrote Lidian just before their marriage, he was born a poet. As he said when he was writing of Goethe, some men are born to write. As he wrote in many places, the most important element in writing is the character and temperament of the man behind the words. He could not have transferred this to his students, though consciously and unconsciously it is what he strove to communicate to all his listeners and readers.

As the best he could offer his students, Emerson would have urged them to develop character of their own, to be themselves, to know themselves, to trust themselves, and to write from that richness.

10

Despite his dependence on privacy, Emerson was social by nature. He missed the kind of London club life he had known in the Athenaeum. The Social Circle was still one of his Concord pleasures, but the Symposium, the Transcendental Club, was long gone. Its membership had dissipated as the movement waned and finally disappeared. A number of the original members had gone off to New York or other cities and careers of their own. Some were dead.

It had not anyway been the kind of club Emerson liked and wished for. The society of overly earnest reformers and humorless "philosophers" often bored and sometimes annoyed him. He preferred men of wit and intelligence, men of culture and polish. As he read "for the lustres"—for the bright, quotable passages that stimulated his mind and imagination—he depended on the talk of cultivated men of experience to "make his top spin."

Emerson had several times suggested to Longfellow, Lowell, and other friends that they organize a club. When he was at home in Concord, he often went into Boston on Saturday mornings. Usually he went to the Boston Athenaeum, the library which his father had helped found.

Sometimes he stopped in at the office of his publishers. He generally went into the Corner Bookshop of Ticknor and Fields at Washington and School Streets.

Then he and a young friend, Samuel Gray Ward, a stockbroker and credit banker with literary tastes, would start seeking a place to lunch. Horatio Woodman, a young lawyer whom they knew, could usually suggest some good inn in the neighborhood. It was Woodman, who cultivated the society of literary men, that pushed the formation of the kind of club Emerson had suggested. Others began to join Emerson, Ward, and him at lunch on Saturdays, first at the Albion Hotel, then at the Revere, later at the Parker House, and the club was an actuality.

At almost the same time, another young man decided to form a club of well-known Boston writers. Francis H. Underwood was what now would be called a "contact man" or public-relations man for the book publishers Phillips and Sampson. Underwood sold his firm the idea of starting a new literary magazine in Boston with New England's leading writers as contributors. The club he started was a method of bringing these writers together for this purpose. Many of these writers were the same men now in the habit of lunching with Emerson on Saturdays. Somehow the two clubs, that formed by Woodman and that formed by Underwood, merged. The Saturday Club, which met to dine at Boston's Parker House on the last Saturday of every month, began in that way.

Its original members included Louis Agassiz, the Swiss naturalist; Richard Henry Dana, Jr., author and lawyer; John Sullivan Dwight, music critic; Emerson; Judge Ebenezer Hoar; James Russell Lowell; John Lothrop Motley, historian; Benjamin Peirce, mathematician and astronomer; Edwin Percy Whipple, literary critic; and Horatio Woodman. These men were soon joined by Hawthorne, Oliver Wendell Holmes, Cornelius Conway Felton, William Hickling Prescott, and John Greenleaf Whittier.

The members of this club were not rustic reformers but men of the world, at least of the world of Boston. Most were from prominent and well-to-do families. Most were Harvard graduates and a number of them, like Holmes, Longfellow, Lowell, Agassiz, and Peirce, taught or had taught at Harvard. Felton was to become Harvard's president. The Club numbered poets, essayists, critics, merchants, politicians, bankers, lawyers, doctors, and scientists. On Emerson's nomination, James Elliot Cabot was made a member. Henry James, Sr., and Charles Sumner, Massachusetts antislavery senator, became members soon afterward. Most of these men had traveled abroad. A number had studied at German or French universities after Harvard. They were men of attainment and, through either birth or accomplishment or both, men of secure position.

Emerson delighted in the meetings of the Saturday Club, which usually began about three o'clock in the afternoon and lasted far into the evening. Agassiz, fat, loud, and cheerful, always sat at one end of the table. Longfellow, florid and dandified, sat at the other. There were no speeches, no formalities. Usually the talk was not general but centered in groups. Emerson, quiet and a little removed as he always seemed, sat near Longfellow, smiled at the jokes, trying, as always, not to laugh outright. He puffed at his cigar and listened more than he spoke. Blue eyes alert, he gathered in the bright remarks. Now and then, with his accustomed poise and grace, he offered his own gentle comments.

When Underwood's dream was realized and *The Atlantic Monthly* was created with Lowell as editor and Holmes as chief contributor, the members of the Saturday Club became its earliest regular writers. *The Dial* had vanished thirteen years before. *The Massachusetts Quarterly Review,* which Theodore Parker had intended as its sturdier successor, had lasted only two years. *The Harbinger,* which

George Ripley had founded as the official publication of Brook Farm, then continued in New York, had died in 1848. Underwood's ambitions were high. He wished the new literary, artistic, and political magazine to be the best that the United States had produced to this time. The quality of the contributors he gathered in the Saturday Club insured its being so.

Emerson contributed twenty-eight pieces of prose or verse to the *Atlantic* during its early years. He was represented in the first issue, November 1857, with four poems: "The Romany Girl," "The Chartist's Complaint," "Days," and "Brahma." All of them were later included in his second volume of poetry, *May-Day and Other Pieces,* 1867.

"The Romany Girl," lyric and pictorial, pleasantly musical, is more colorful and lightly romantic than most of Emerson's poetry.

> The sun goes down and with him takes
> The coarseness of my poor attire;
> The fair moon mounts, and aye the flame
> Of Gypsy beauty blazes higher.
>
> Pale Northern girls! you scorn our race;
> You captives of your air-tight halls,
> Wear out indoors your sickly days,
> But leave us the horizon walls. . . .
>
> Go, keep your cheek's rose from the rain,
> For teeth and hair with shopmen deal;
> My swarthy tint is in the grain,
> The rocks and forest know it real.

"Days" is one of the most popular of Emerson's poems, reprinted in many anthologies. The image is consistent and effective. The Emersonian moral is clear: expect and exact the most of yourself. Of all his poems, this was Emerson's favorite.

Daughters of Time, the hypocritic Days,
Muffled and dumb, like barefoot dervishes,
And marching single in an endless file,
Bring diadems and fagots in their hands.
To each they offer gifts after his will,
Bread, kingdoms, stars, and sky that holds them all.
I, in my pleached garden, watched the pomp,
Forgot my morning wishes, hastily
Took a few herbs and apples, and the Day
Turned and departed silent. I, too late,
Under her solemn fillet saw the scorn.

"Brahma" is fundamental Emerson. In the Hindu religion, which fascinated him, Brahma is the supreme soul or essence of the universe. He is changeless and eternal. Some readers found the poem, which begins, "If the red slayer think he slays," hard to understand. Emerson thought it was very clear. His point was that every man, depending on whether he follows good or evil, saves or slays himself.

Out of the Saturday Club, and in the same year which saw the founding of the *Atlantic,* grew yet another club. William J. Stillman, a painter friend of Lowell's and of Charles Eliot Norton, another Harvard professor who was elected to the Saturday Club in 1860, was an outdoor enthusiast who loved the Adirondack mountains of his native New York. Stillman persuaded Lowell, and Lowell in turn persuaded other members of the Saturday Club, to buy a wilderness tract of more than a thousand acres in the Adirondacks.

In August 1858 the Adirondack Club, with Stillman as leader and chief guide, camped out by a spring at the head of Follansbee Pond. They slept under a roof of pine bark laid on a ridgepole between two giant maples. Holmes had refused to go. He was too much the dainty Bostonian and disliked raw nature. Longfellow had debated going, but he was cautious. He asked Stillman if it were true that Emerson had bought a gun for the trip. When Stillman answered that it was, Longfellow made up his mind: "Then I shall not go; somebody will be shot."

Agassiz, Emerson, Stillman, Judge Hoar, Lowell, Woodman, several others, and three guides made up the party. Emerson shot off his gun, but only—as Thoreau complained when he heard about it—at beer-bottle targets. When one of the guides paddled him out on the lake jack-hunting for deer at night, a deer was drawn to the shore by the torchlight the guide held up. He whispered excitedly to Emerson to shoot. Emerson did not. He could not.

On a previous visit with Stillman, Lowell had shot a bear that was swimming across the lake. This time he climbed a tall white pine to reach an osprey's nest. It was empty. Lowell tried several times to shoot the osprey which circled about the nest, but failed.

Emerson felt overpowered by the great forest. Several times he had himself rowed to secluded spots along the lake shore, where he stayed with his thoughts and emotions. He talked to the guides, whom he saw as self-sufficient foresters. He talked to Stillman. Stillman was the kind of well-rounded, capable man, skilled in woodcraft as well as in his art as a painter, whom Emerson most admired. To Stillman, Emerson with his serenity stood out from all the other adventurers. Emerson seemed to him to represent universal humanity. Stillman painted the camp and campers with Emerson standing by himself near a huge tree, watching a group of the others fire at a target fastened to the trunk of a smaller tree. Judge Hoar bought the painting which, at his death, went to the Concord Free Public Library, which still owns it.

The next summer Emerson remained in Concord. It proved more dangerous than the Adirondacks. On a walk to Wachusett he sprained his foot. One doctor told him that it needed splints and absolute rest. A second said to rest the foot but not to put it in splints. A third told him not to rest the foot at all but to get out and walk and so work out the lameness. One of them advised him to pour warm water on the foot; another, to stand in a cold trout brook. Which cure Emerson adopted he does not say. Presumably nature came to the rescue, and his foot got well of itself.

For Emerson, the Saturday Club, the Adirondack Club, the Social Circle, and his walks and talks about Concord were the pleasures and diversions of busy years marred by the increasing bitterness of the antislavery struggle and the sectional strains and conflicts which led to the Civil War.

Emerson had always voted dutifully, but he had felt until this time only a nominal interest in public life and had had no desire to participate in it. At twenty-three he had attended funeral ceremonies for John Adams and Thomas Jefferson, both of whom died in 1826. Daniel Webster, then the admired of all New England, had delivered the oration in Boston's Faneuil Hall, and Emerson had been impressed by his eloquence. When James Monroe died in 1831, Emerson noted dryly in his journal, "President Monroe died on the fourth of July,—a respectable man, I believe."

He dined with John Quincy Adams two weeks later and in August heard his host deliver a eulogy on Monroe. Emerson found nothing heroic in the subject and little in the feelings of the speaker. Emerson admired the military energy of Andrew Jackson during his presidency but despised the presidents who, like James K. Polk, fought the Mexican War to expand slave territory or, like Franklin Pierce, supported the Kansas-Nebraska Bill. This permitted settlers in those territories to decide whether or not they would countenance slavery.

Greater awareness of political America had come to Emerson with his westward travels, his widening acquaintance with new and larger parts of the country, and with the rise of slavery from a difference of opinion between

153

parties and sections into a burning issue that was to blaze into war.

The Saturday Club itself was split by dissension. Emerson felt that Hawthorne's friendship for his college mate and political benefactor, "that paltry Franklin Pierce," was unfortunate. Felton was a proslavery Whig. Sumner was a militant fighter against slavery. In 1856, Sumner, on the Senate floor, violently attacked Senator Andrew Pickens Butler of South Carolina in his speech "The Crime Against Kansas." Two days later, while seated at his desk, Sumner was brutally and almost fatally attacked with a stout walking stick by a congressman nephew of the Southern senator. Permanently injured, Sumner was forced to be absent from the Senate for three and a half years.

Emerson had never been a militant Abolitionist. He was not even as strong an antislavery man as Alcott or Thoreau. Emerson abhorred slavery, but his principles had been tempered by his common sense and what he had observed in his travels. He did not believe the Negro was prepared for social and political independence. He did not advocate the overthrow of slavery by violence. What he did advocate was freeing the slaves by purchasing them from their owners.

He spoke out now in favor of this scheme, urging it as a solution no matter if it cost the billions it was said it would take, and billions of dollars were considered staggering sums in pre-Civil War years. With other bitter New Englanders he turned against Daniel Webster because he had supported the Fugitive Slave Act, which made it mandatory for everyone to aid in the capture and return of runaway slaves. Emerson demanded that this Act be abrogated and wiped off the books. He said that Webster, once the pride of New England, was now its mortification.

In a speech in Concord, Emerson said that either the country had to get rid of slavery or get rid of freedom. This was after the attack on Charles Sumner. Emerson spoke at Kansas relief meetings and even supported sending arms to help Kansas resist proslavery raids from Missouri. When John Brown of Kansas spoke in the Concord town hall, Emerson thought he gave a good account of himself. When Brown was captured and imprisoned after his ineffectual raid on Harpers Ferry, Emerson spoke out in his defense. While Brown awaited execution, Emerson called him a new saint facing martyrdom.

Emerson spoke against slavery at Harvard, where conservative sentiment was for maintaining things as they were and the college authorities were known to be on the side of the South. The Harvard students interrupted his speech with hisses and catcalls. Emerson simply stood quietly on the platform and waited for the booing to cease, then continued as if nothing had happened. A spectator reported that this action heightened indescribably the effect of what he said.

Emerson hailed Lincoln's election as "sublime, the pronunciation of the masses against slavery." He lectured in Washington in 1862, and Lincoln may have been in the audience, for he spoke later of having heard Emerson speak. When the Emancipation Proclamation was released in September 1862, Emerson was deeply moved. He wrote his "Boston Hymn," reading it in Boston's Music Hall, January 1, 1863, when the Proclamation became effective. God is speaking in these two of the Hymn's twenty-two stanzas:

I break your bonds and masterships,
And I unchain the slave:
Free be his heart and hand henceforth
As wind and wandering wave. . . .

To-day unbind the captive,
So only are ye unbound;
Lift up a people from the dust,
Trump of their rescue, sound!

155

During the war Emerson gave one unscheduled and very brief speech in Concord. Julian Hawthorne, then a boy, was present and remembered it all his life. The war was going badly for the North when the Concord town meeting was held. Union armies had suffered severe defeats. Men from Concord had been killed, and feelings ran high. One man in the crowd leaped suddenly to his feet and screamed out that another present was a Copperhead, a treacherous Northerner who sympathized with the South and was secretly working for the enemy.

The accused man bowed his head over his knees where he sat and covered his face with his hands. His sixteen-year-old daughter, seated next to him, began to sob in terror. The accuser harangued the meeting, and violence threatened as the angered crowd took on the aspects of a mob.

Making his way up the aisle through his shouting and gesticulating townsmen, Emerson faced them from the platform. For what seemed to young Hawthorne a long time, he just stood there. He made no movement, did not speak. Gradually the confusion lessened and the room grew quiet as people stared at him. Emerson said nothing until only the sobbing of the terrified girl could be heard. Then he spoke slowly and distinctly, making his ringing voice heard in every corner of the room.

"Is this—Concord?" he asked. The riot and possible bloodshed were averted.

Emerson's admiration for Abraham Lincoln grew. They met February 2, 1862, when Senator Charles Sumner took Emerson to call on Chase, Stanton, Welles, Seward, and the President. Immediately afterward Emerson wrote in his journal: "The President impressed me more favourably than I had hoped. A frank, sincere, well-meaning man, with a lawyer's habit of mind, good clear statement of his fact; correct enough, not vulgar, as described, but with a sort of boyish cheerfulness, or that kind of sincerity and

Emerson met Abraham Lincoln, February 2, 1862.

157

jolly good meaning that our class meetings on Commencement Days show, in telling our stories over. When he has made his remark, he looks up at you with great satisfaction, and shows all his white teeth, and laughs."

The next year Lincoln appointed Emerson one of the Board of Visitors to the United States Military Academy at West Point. At the Point, where Emerson spent more than two weeks examining teaching procedures and their results, he was much impressed by the cadets' air of truthfulness and loyalty to each other. He approved of their being taught French, mathematics, geology, tactics, engineering, swimming, and dancing, but he thought that science should be stressed in the Academy's curriculum.

As for everyone else, the Civil War was a difficult time for Emerson. People were fighting, not reading. The income from his books vanished. As wartime travel was difficult and impossible in some places, his income from lecturing also suffered. Yet Emerson wished for no hasty peace, "or any peace restoring the old rottenness."

Emerson suffered more personal losses during the war. Aunt Mary had disparaged his early lectures and writing. She had not even approved of the *Essays*. Finally she admitted that if he had been, according to her lights, more truly religious, he could have written *Paradise Lost* without the dull parts. She could give her nephew no higher praise.

For nearly four years, senile, a wreck of her former self, as even Emerson admitted, she had been living under the care of a niece in the Williamsburg section of Brooklyn. For years she had been prepared for death and talked rapturously and eagerly of her anticipation of it, but she was nearly eighty-nine years old when she died in Williamsburg in May 1863. She had pleaded to be buried in Concord. Though once she had sworn never to enter his house again, it was near her nephew in Concord's Sleepy Hollow Cemetery that she wished to lie.

After the funeral, Emerson offered her papers to other

158

family members. No one wanted them. He did. Six years later he read long extracts from his Aunt Mary's journal to an audience of women in Boston and unstintedly acknowledged his lasting debt to the sharp-tongued and rudely demanding little eccentric who had been so important in his life. Mary Moody Emerson had been fantastic, and he said so. She had been as prickly as a porcupine in her independence: "She could keep step with no human being"; yet her quick mind and her apt, sharp phrases had been an inspiration to him always.

Over the years a coolness had developed between Emerson and Thoreau, though they remained friends. Truculent and rigid, Thoreau resented Emerson's patronage. Perhaps unconsciously he resented the success that seemed to attend everything Emerson attempted. He disliked the formality of manner which, whether on the platform or when they walked together, Emerson could not doff. It seemed to proud Thoreau that they never met as equals. Thoreau thought Emerson cold. He disapproved of Emerson's concessions to the polite world, concessions which Thoreau could or would never attempt.

Emerson had got a little impatient with Thoreau's literalness, his refusal to meet life on other than his own terms, his unnecessary pugnacity in debate. He had found and treasured Thoreau as a rough diamond. He was disappointed that after all the years the diamond refused to take a polish. He liked and admired Henry Thoreau, whom twice he had taken into his home for long periods and for whom he had worked hard to find editors, publishers, and readers, but there were times when he found him ungracious and insufferable. Emerson thought Thoreau cold.

After a long and wasting illness, Thoreau died of tuberculosis May 6, 1862. He was forty-four years old.

Emerson delivered the funeral address, which was a tribute to Thoreau's honesty and independence, to his integrity, above all to his Indianlike stoicism and his kinship with nature. In his address, which was published in expanded form in *The Atlantic Monthly* the following summer, Emerson made known what have since become well-known quotations from Thoreau's journals. These he saw for the first time after Thoreau's death and helped Thoreau's sister Sophia to edit. Toward the end of his life Emerson remembered Henry Thoreau as one who stood out on the list of those he called "my men," but he seemed more disturbed at the time of its happening by the death of another of his Concord neighbors.

Nathaniel Hawthorne, who had returned to Concord in 1860 after four years as American consul in Liverpool and another two years in Italy, died in May 1864. Emerson was deeply distressed. Though they had had one long and happy walk together, he felt he had never really got to know the silent Hawthorne. Despite *The Scarlet Letter* and *The House of the Seven Gables,* he thought that Hawthorne had never achieved the writing of which he was capable. He was convinced that Hawthorne was a greater man than any of his work showed him, and had been determined to know him better. He had thought there would be time for that. Now there was none.

With other members of The Saturday Club, Emerson served as a pallbearer, following the hearse from the Concord church, which had been decorated with white flowers, to Sleepy Hollow Cemetery, where Ellen, Waldo, his Aunt Mary, and Henry Thoreau all lay buried.

11

Even before the long and bitter Civil War was over, Emerson took to the road again. Night after winter night he appeared on the lecture platform in New England, in New York, and throughout the Middle West. New audiences gave the famous speaker the same rapt attention that earlier audiences had given him before the war.

Countenance lighted, blue eyes clear, voice resonant and musical, Emerson spoke with all the charm and quiet emphasis that had fascinated listeners for years. Whatever his subject, they heard Emerson and were thrilled by a presence that rose over and above anything and everything he said.

His subjects were the old ones, or new ones little changed from the old. He spoke on Social Aims; Books, Poetry, and Criticism; American Life; American Character; Success; Culture; Immortality. One season Emerson would offer this selection from his rich portfolio; the next season, he would select and rearrange others for his annual tour.

Emerson enjoyed seeing new places, revisiting old ones. He was always interested in people, all kinds, and he saw many kinds on his travels. Yet there were the old trials of travel, and these were varied by new vexations. Once, after giving two lectures in Toronto, Canada, and visiting Niagara Falls, he went early to bed in the American House in Rochester. At three in the morning he was awakened by cries of "Fire!" Grabbing his possessions and yanking on what clothes he could, he ran into the smoke-filled hall and through smoke and cinders down the stairs to the street. There with other freezing guests he watched the hotel burn. He had lost his ticket from Buffalo to Chicago. A Detroit railroad man gave him a pass over his road.

Once in Illinois when the temperature was twenty-two below zero, Emerson took to his bed. It was the only refuge he could find against the prairie winter. What seemed even worse at the time was that his shirts did not fit. It was only a petty annoyance, he wrote his wife, but it caused him a great deal of trouble. It was disconcerting when he arrived late before a lecture to find his shirts were too small to button at the neck, and he could not stay in one place long enough to have his wardrobe mended.

The mails were uncertain and usually late. Emerson was continually missing letters from home. He tried his best to keep his itinerary, always complicated by last-minute changes, straight for his family. He would be in Indianapolis or Detroit, or whatever the place, on such and such dates, then on to somewhere else and from somewhere else to elsewhere—Chicago, St. Louis, Keokuk, Des Moines, Independence, Cedar Falls, Quincy, Bloomington.

Everywhere he spoke with his consummate skill. Though he read his lectures, it seemed as if his vividly blue eyes were continually on his audience, except when he searched the walls or the ceiling for a quotation he wished to recall. Sometimes he told a joke to stress a point, though these were taken out when the lecture or the essay based on it was published. Emerson stood motionless on the platform, though occasionally his body swayed forward as he under-

162

lined a point. His face, his gentleness, his voice were all the gestures he needed.

Moncure Conway, a young Methodist circuit rider from Virginia who became a Unitarian minister in the North, thought Emerson at his best with small audiences who knew and loved him in and around Concord. Yet Conway describes the dramatic effect of Emerson's words and presence on an audience of five thousand one Sunday morning in the Boston Music Hall. Emerson's subject was religion, all religions. As always, he counseled seeking the inner light within one's own soul. Quietly he told a story to illustrate his meaning. Then, as quietly, he gathered up his notes, smiled, and sat down. Many of his listeners were in tears. For moments after he was seated the assemblage of thousands sat in spellbound silence.

In 1865 he spoke at Pittsburgh. He talked in Cleveland on "Social Aims in America." In Milwaukee on successive January nights he spoke on "Education," "Social Aims," "Table Talk," "Books," and "Character." Then he repeated this same series in Chicago. That fall he gave a series of lectures at Amherst and spoke in Northampton, which, he wrote his daughter Ellen, he considered the most beautiful town in Massachusetts. The next season he was writing his family—almost always enclosing drafts of the money paid him for his lecturing—from towns and cities in Illinois, Michigan, Indiana, and Ohio, as he moved from one to another to speak in lecture halls, colleges, and churches.

To his delight, his younger daughter, Edith, married Lieutenant Colonel William H. Forbes in October 1865. He was the son of John Murray Forbes, the wealthy railroad builder and public spirited "Squire of Naushon" on Buzzards Bay, whom Emerson greatly admired. After this, it was usually to Ellen that he sent his letters from La Porte, Davenport, Battle Creek, Ann Arbor, Toledo, Columbus, Fond du Lac, Peoria, St. Louis, Erie, and points among and between.

He wrote that he had stayed up all night the night before in a railroad station—that he was snug and safe in a hotel with the temperature below zero outside—that he had received a letter from her mother and another from Edward—that she would please use the enclosed to pay off his note at the bank—that he would like to have Edward pay three dollars to a Boston shop for the last soft hat he had bought.

Honors began to come to Emerson now. For thirty years he had been anathema to the authorities at Harvard. The words are his son's. Shocked Harvard had ostracized him after "The Divinity School Address," but Emerson was no longer the renegade preacher proposing what the ultra-conservative saw as heretical religious doctrines. He was no longer the ridiculed "Transcendentalist." He was the most eminent writer in America. Poet, essayist, lecturer, friend and associate of the great, admired in Europe as well as in the United States, he had achieved an established success. It was safe for a younger and more liberal-minded generation of Harvard authorities to accept him now.

Harvard bestowed the honorary degree of Doctor of Laws on its well-beloved son, Ralph Waldo Emerson, in 1866. In 1867, just thirty years after he had delivered "The American Scholar," he was asked again to give Harvard's Phi Beta Kappa oration. He spoke on "The Progress of Culture." He was made an Overseer of Harvard this same year and served until 1879. In 1869 Emerson gave a long series of readings from the English poets before large Boston audiences. In 1870 he gave a course of lectures in philosophy to a class of thirty students at Harvard, and repeated the course the following year. The course was an effort for him. Emerson had always disliked trying to array his thoughts in methodical order. It was getting more difficult for him as he grew older. The Harvard course tired him. He was glad to take a long trip into new scenes when the course, which became a book, *Natural History of Intellect,* was finished.

In 1871, John Murray Forbes saw that Emerson was tired. He made up a party consisting of his son, his daughter-in-law, and a few others, and took Emerson in his private Pullman car off to distant California. It was Emerson's first glimpse of the grandeur of the Far West, and he was awed by it. When the party traveled by wagon and on horseback up the Yosemite Valley, he rode with loose rein, paying no attention to his mount, his eyes fixed on the mountains. An experienced traveler, he accepted cheerfully the discomforts which dismayed the others. Entranced by what he saw, he sometimes rode in the wagon with a heavy buffalo robe over his knees, though the sun's heat was intense.

In San Francisco, Emerson visited the opium dens, gazing at the rows of stupefied Chinese on their shelflike bunks. He spoke on "Immortality," the first time he ever addressed a California audience. On the return journey he met and talked with the Mormon prophet, Brigham Young, in thriving Salt Lake City.

Like most men, Emerson was of two minds about some things. His son, Edward, was just returning from a trip and Emerson just starting out for one of his western tours when they met to spend one winter night in the St. Denis Hotel in New York. Emerson read his son some of the poems which were soon to be published in *May-Day and Other Pieces.* One of the "other pieces" was "Terminus."

It is time to be old,
To take in sail:—
The god of bounds,
Who sets to seas a shore,
Came to me in his fatal rounds,
And said: "No more!
No farther shoot
Thy broad ambitious branches, and thy root." . . .

His father looked so alive, so forceful and young in spirit, that Edward Emerson was startled. "Terminus" sounded like a confession that he knew his powers were failing.

Emerson did not often feel they were. In his early sixties he wrote in his journal, "Within I do not find wrinkles and used heart, but unspent youth." In spirit, Emerson never aged. In mind and body he did age, and in 1872 he received a shock from which he never fully recovered.

Emerson returned July 24 from still another lecture engagement in Amherst. None of his children were at home. Ellen was vacationing at the shore; Edith and her husband were en route back from Europe; Edward was studying medicine at St. Thomas Hospital in London. Emerson and his wife went quietly to bed.

They were awakened early the next morning by flames licking through the floor of a closet in a room above them. Half-dressed, they fled outdoors into a hard rain. By this time the fire was well under way. Neighbors rushed to their assistance and dragged and pushed through the doors and out the windows all the Emerson possessions they could save. The whole upper part of the house was burning now.

Working fast, friends tumbled Emerson's books and pictures out of the burning house, and Louisa May Alcott, now a woman of forty and famous as the author of *Little Women*, stood guard over them. Calm through all the excitement, though he was chilled and wet, Emerson told her that he now saw his library in a new light—and asked if she knew where the neighbors had flung his boots.

The house was badly damaged. The Emersons went to live once more in the Old Manse. A temporary study was set up for him in the Concord Court House. Everything was done to ease his discomfort, but the shock and exposure had been too much for the sixty-nine-year-old Emerson. He said that on the morning after the fire he had felt something snap in his brain. He grew severely ill.

166

The Emerson home burned July 25, 1872.

Friends rushed to his assistance. One insisted he accept a gift of $5,000. Another, LeBaron Russell, told a score more who loved and venerated Emerson that they could help. These subscribed another $12,000. The plan was to rebuild the Emerson house exactly as it had been and to send him abroad to recover while the work was being done. Ill and feeble, Emerson was nearly overcome anew. "Are my friends bent on killing me with kindness?" he asked Russell in a letter of October 8, 1872. ". . . I thought myself sufficiently loaded with benefits already, and you add more and more."

That month, with his daughter Ellen, Emerson sailed for England. The shock of the fire had caused all his brown hair to fall out. Moncure Conway, who by this time was a Unitarian minister in London, says that when Emerson landed in England his head was completely hairless, like a baby's. When Emerson and his daughter returned to England in the spring of 1873 after traveling through Italy, thence to Egypt, and up the Nile, his head was covered with white hair a half-inch long.

Emerson and Ellen stayed with James Russell Lowell in Paris. In England he saw Carlyle and other friends once more. He lunched with Lord Russell. Once more he was accorded the privileges of the Athenaeum. Going up to Oxford, he met John Ruskin; Benjamin Jowett, Greek scholar and Master of Balliol; and Charles Dodgson, the Oxford mathematician who as Lewis Carroll wrote *Alice in Wonderland.*

Father and daughter sailed for home May 3. When they arrived in Concord, all the bells of the town were ringing. Hundreds of school children met them at the railroad station, singing "Home, Sweet Home." A crowd of cheering townspeople escorted them home through a floral arch of triumph. The handsome square house, newly rebuilt and painted, looked as if it had never been disturbed. Inside, all Emerson's books and pictures were in place as they had been before the fire.

Too moved to speak, Emerson started to enter the house. At the door he turned and went back to the white gate where the crowd of smiling friends stood and watched. "My friends!" he said, "I know this is not a tribute to an old man and his daughter returning to their house, but to the common blood of us all—one family—in Concord!"

Emerson tried to take up his full life again, but he could no longer live and work with his old vigor. He had to limit his travels. He continued to lecture, but his memory was failing, and he had difficulty finding the words he wished. A member of the family had to be close at hand to help him find his place in his manuscript. As if the faculty he had most exercised in his long career were the first to wear out, it was Emerson's memory for words, especially for names, that left him.

New honors were bestowed on him. In 1874 he was nominated for the Lord Rectorship of the University of Glasgow in Scotland and received five hundred votes. Benjamin Disraeli, novelist and England's Prime Minister, won with seven hundred. Emerson was made an Associate Member of the French Academy in 1875. As his name and fame continued to increase, there was a strong and rising demand for his books. Humorously, Emerson decided that old age was a good advertisement. "Your name has been seen so often that your book must be worth buying."

His publishers pressed for new work which it was impossible for him to do. He could no longer select and order material from his journals and lectures and compose a finished book. It was a great relief to him when James Elliot Cabot, whom he made his literary executor, undertook to prepare his *Letters and Social Aims* for publication in 1876.

Emerson accepted eagerly when he was invited to speak

at the University of Virginia in 1876. The result was catastrophic. It was too soon after the war for a Southern audience to listen patiently to a Yankee idealist who obviously was no longer at the height of his great powers. The audience became restive soon after he began to talk. People began to whisper to each other, then to converse aloud, ignoring the speaker. Only at Harvard when he spoke against slavery had Emerson been greeted with comparable rudeness. When the noise and talk mounted, Emerson quietly brought his lecture on "The Scholar" to a close and left the platform. Not even to close friends did he complain afterward of his reception in Charlottesville.

Gradually Emerson ceased attending the dinners of the Saturday Club. He could no longer join in general conversation without embarrassment at being unable to reach into his mind and produce the right word. Physically, Emerson looked well and was well. He was as gentle and seemingly as unperturbed as always. Simply he was silent, speaking only in brief sentences or with a word or two when he could. He could laugh at his infirmity and talk of his "naughty memory," which amused when it did not annoy him, but even simple words eluded him. He had to describe in roundabout fashion what he meant. A chair became "that which supports the human frame," and a plow "the implement that cultivates the soil."

Because he could listen without having to participate, he went more often to lectures and to church. He enjoyed his walks and his gardens and the visits of close friends. As was his custom, he took the train back and forth to Boston, friends, whom often he did not recognize, keeping a watchful eye out for his safety.

The swift spirit had slowed and the winged words faltered. The blazing ambition of the young man and his zealous Aunt Mary had been quenched by achievement. Emerson was replete. He made his last public appearance

170

in Boston in February 1881 when he read a paper on Carlyle, who had just died at eighty-six. Bronson Alcott, even older than he and sometimes billed now as "Dr. Brunson [sic] Alcott, The Concord Sage and Gifted Sire of Louisa M. Alcott, Authoress of *Little Women*, etc.," had opened his Concord School of Philosophy in 1879. Emerson read a paper on "Aristocracy" before it in the spring of 1881. He had spoken one hundred times to Concord audiences.

Henry Wadsworth Longfellow died toward the end of March 1882. Oliver Wendell Holmes, who sat opposite Emerson at the funeral, says that Emerson rose, went to the coffin, and peered intently at the face of his dead friend. A few minutes later, evidently forgetting that he had already done so, he repeated the action. Then he said, "That gentleman was a sweet, beautiful soul, but I have completely forgotten his name."

A few weeks later, Emerson caught cold and fell asleep on the sofa in his study. When he awoke, he was feverish and bewildered. His son, now a physician practicing in Concord, read him "Paul Revere's Ride." Emerson was as delighted as a child with the familiar story, which he was sure he had never heard before. He did not know Longfellow or his poem, but he knew Carlyle, if not his name. He pointed to a bust of Carlyle, saying, "That is my man, my good man!"

The next day pneumonia developed. Emerson knew that he was very ill and that probably he would die. He insisted on being dressed and sitting in his study. Most of the time during his brief final illness he sat in a chair by his fire. He ate and drank little. He was in no pain.

Friends came to see him, and he tried to talk with them. He said goodbye to several on his last day, the only day that he spent entirely in bed. When pain struck at the very last, he was given sedatives. Ralph Waldo Emerson died Thursday evening, April 27, 1882.

12

In the end, the events of a man's life are unimportant. It is what he is and what he does, the record that he leaves of his mind and heart, that matter. So Emerson believed.

"Great geniuses have the shortest biographies," he wrote in *Representative Men*. "Their cousins can tell you nothing about them. They lived in their writings, and so their house and street life was trivial and commonplace. . . . Plato especially has no external biography. If he had lover, wife, or children, we hear nothing of them. He ground them all into paint. . . . As a good chimney burns its smoke, so a philosopher converts the value of all his fortunes into his intellectual performances."

Emerson, too, ground them all into paint: his Boston boyhood, his brothers, Harvard, the Second Church, Ellen Tucker, Thoreau, the humble-bee in the woods, Napoleon, Concord, the American West, the rhodora. His thoughts and feelings about people and things, all that he lived and experienced, became the substance of his books. A thoughtful writer is always more himself in his writings than he is in his person or in his day-to-day life with other people. His essential character is in his work. The real Emerson

172

is in his lectures, his essays, his poems, and his journal, but even the total of these does not equal the complete Emerson.

The tall, thin figure in black looked sometimes the villager he was when, top hat in hand, he walked up the aisle to the speaker's platform. When he had placed the hat somewhere behind him, arranged the pages of his lecture on the desk or table before him, and faced his audience, he was transfigured. He seemed less man than spirit. When he began to speak, the tones of his voice thrilled his listeners. They felt transformed, elevated, and ennobled by his presence and his simple belief that they shared his high thoughts.

The Concord blacksmith, the Boston clerk, the prairie farmer did not always understand everything that Emerson said, but they felt that he was sharing with them the best there was. The man's essential goodness reached through to them, and they felt they breathed a higher and purer air. One unlettered housewife of Concord went to hear Emerson as often as she could. The intellectual reaches of his talk were beyond her, but not the homely, everyday illustrations he used, and she said she liked to see Mr. Emerson standing up there as if he thought everyone were as good as he was.

Highly educated and gifted men and women were equally fascinated, though not always for the same reasons. The English novelist Anthony Trollope heard Emerson speak for the first time when he addressed a large audience during the Civil War. Trollope had heard that Emerson was sometimes obscure and difficult to follow. He was amazed to find him instead clear-sighted, bold, frank, and practical. Trollope saw that Emerson commanded his listeners' respect by his utter honesty.

In *English Traits*, Emerson noted that the English like to put a solid bar of sleep between each day and the next. He did too. When he got up, he wanted pie, apple pie or blueberry if he could get it, for breakfast. It was an old New England custom that he enjoyed. A lone traveler in many places, he liked to do things for himself. Even in his last illness, he insisted on raking the coals and setting the fire in his hearth for the night. He liked to be warm. After a cold and arduous trip he would enter an inn far from Concord, smile, and say to the desk clerk, "Now make me warm, please!"

The tastes of the man who had wined and dined with lords and ladies in London, talked with Carlyle and walked with Wordsworth, were simple. He was never happier than when at work with hatchet and shears in his woodlot or when, twirling his favorite stick, he strolled to Walden Pond, Baker Farm, the Columbine Rock, or some other favorite spot about Concord on his afternoon walk.

On a higher plane, his tastes were as simple and as universal. He loved God. He loved truth and beauty. He loved the possibilities for knowing God and goodness and beauty that are in the human soul. In his lectures and in his books, he told men and women about this in words and in a way which made them feel his own spiritual uplift and share his hopes. The English poet and critic Matthew Arnold called him the friend of all those who would live in the spirit.

That was where Emerson lived. He did not live in his mind and concoct foolproof schemes for existence. Simply he taught men that there is a knowledge in the untaught human spirit on which they can rely. He told them that there is God in man that corresponds to, is part of, God that resides in all nature. Man, he said, had but to trust himself to feel and know this.

Emerson did not attempt to explain the how or the why of the truths he believed and uttered. He presented not conclusions but visions. He spoke from the universal human hunger for universal spiritual experience. He reassured his listeners and readers of their own worth as individual

174

human beings. He talked to them in vivid and telling phrases, with the sound of music and the play of light through his words, and these wrought their own enchantment.

Emerson was a man of the world, but at the same time he was very much a man of Concord. He could converse as an equal with the learned, and dine as one of them with the doctors of Harvard. He could move great Boston audiences to tears and inspire young men and women in snowbound prairie towns. Yet he preferred to do his own work in his own woodlot and to eat his own pie at his own breakfast table. There was something that was exalted about Emerson, but there was also much that was plain and practical.

Carlyle had seen the face of an angel in the young man. That saintlike look clung to Emerson all his life, but the spare figure in black on the streets of Boston, or in gray with a soft hat in Concord and the country, was to many just a respected if bookish neighbor. They liked him, not because he was a famous author and a celebrated speaker, but because he was a fair-dealing, common-sense New Englander who kept his house, orchards, and fields in good order and spoke his own mind.

Like Thoreau, whose mentor he was, Emerson despised the masses and valued the individual. The masses were stupid and usually wrong. They mattered only as they were made up of individuals who could rise above the level of the mass. In religion, in politics, everywhere in life, it was personal freedom that mattered to Emerson.

Thoreau obtained this freedom by withdrawing from the ordinary pursuits of practical life. He followed no profession. He did not vote. He built his own world at Walden Pond and in his heart. Emerson remained in the hard, competitive, practical world. He was a man among men in the ordinary life of his day. He maintained his freedom by doing what he advised in "Self-Reliance." In the midst of the crowd he maintained with perfect sweetness the independence of solitude.

He went to bed at ten o'clock at night. He rose at six in the morning and went about his business. It just happened that his business was man's spirit. He was sometimes courteously aloof to people about him because his thoughts were elsewhere. It was not in his "farming" or in his preaching, in his teaching or in arranging for his lectures and other necessary business, that he really lived. Emerson lived in his writing. His real life was there. He was formal in speech and manner. He was exhilarated in his writing. There is no aloofness there. In prose or in verse, his words are vibrant with the man's full life.

Emerson wrote essays that are compact of wisdom and poetry. They still convey with freshness his delight in nature and in thought. In 1907 George Edward Woodberry wrote, "His is the only great mind that America has produced in literature." After the passage of more than a half-century, this still seems a sound judgment. As Woodberry pointed out, Emerson convinces men of his greatness. His materials were permanent. His subjects are what thoughtful men and women have thought about since men and women have thought at all. Neither time nor place affects Emerson's writings. Emerson wrote about what is universal in human spiritual experience. His words are as fresh and as significant in Europe or Africa as in the United States, as alive and inspiriting now as when he wrote them. There is about them a permeating nobility of thought and expression which is unmistakable and lasting.

Emerson was a poet. The sense of wonder never died in him. He was a poet who in his prose as well as in his verse used words with a poet's delight in their sound and color, used them with a poet's insight to convey what Thoreau called the hue and fragrance of the thought. He was a poet in his perpetual endeavor to penetrate appearances and to express the spirit of the thing. When he dared define it at

176

all, it was this endeavor he defined as the attempt of all poetry.

Yet it was not all poetry with Emerson. There was a dry humor in his speech and often in his writing. He could disconcert with common sense, his was so simply sensible. At the same time, he could surprise and delight with the uncommon sense of a gifted mind and pen. There is steel in Emerson, but there is music too. He liked the hardwoods, oak, maple, beech, but he loved the soft and fragrant pines. He noted once that men like the hardwoods; women, pitch-pines. Emerson was the most masculine of men in his independence and courage, but there was a touch of the feminine, too, in his intuitions and perceptions.

Emerson loved the rhodora as a thing of beauty. He loved all beauty. He also loved pie. Once at breakfast in company he offered a piece of his favorite pie to first one, then another, only to have them all refuse with something of a shudder. Emerson thrust his knife under a generous wedge and asked with humorous gravity, "But what is pie for?" His message was as simple.

True to an impulse he first felt as truth in the marrow of his bones and the sinews of his brain, he was himself. He wanted others to be themselves. He did not wish anyone else to be Emerson. He wished John Smith to be John Smith and Mary Jones to be Mary Jones.

Emerson loved a priest of whatever persuasion. Yet he abandoned the pastorate of a denominational congregation to embrace a larger religion of the human spirit. He felt akin to the Quakers; he was drawn to Hinduism as well as to Christianity. He felt at one with Roman Catholicism. After attending Mass in the cathedral in Baltimore, he wrote his wife of the dignity he felt where "the priest is nothing and the people nothing" but God is everything. Deeply moved, he wrote, ". . . to-day I detest the Uni-tarians and Martin Luther and all the parliament of Bare-bones."

177

Again, he wrote Lidian that it was well for his Protestantism that there was no cathedral in Concord: "I should be confirmed in a fortnight." When he heard that a young woman of a rich and decorous Unitarian family in Boston was about to join the Roman Catholic Church, Emerson told lamenting friends that he was delighted, provided she had been truly drawn to it by "its beautiful forms and humane spirit." Emerson was descended from seven generations of Puritan divines. He had been trained in Unitarian doctrine at the Harvard Divinity School. Yet he was more in accord with the liberal sentiments of organized religion of a later century than with the narrower sectarian views of his own time.

The reason for his attitude was simple. It was the same simple reason which underlay all his thought. He spoke it many times in many ways, and once again when he said, "Nothing is at last sacred but the integrity of our own mind."

RALPH WALDO EMERSON

1803—Born May 25 in Boston.

1817—Entered Harvard College.

1820—Began to keep his journal.

1821—Graduated from Harvard.
　　　Began to teach school.

1825—Entered Harvard Divinity School.

1826—Licensed to preach.
　　　Went to Florida for his health.

1829—Ordained assistant minister of Second Church, Boston, March 11; soon became its minister.
　　　Married Ellen Louisa Tucker, September 30.

1831—Ellen Tucker Emerson died February 8.

1832—Resigned pulpit of Second Church, September 9.
　　　Sailed for Europe, December 25.

1833—Met Landor, Wordsworth, Coleridge, and Carlyle abroad.

1834—Edward Emerson, brother, died in Porto Rico, October 1.

1835—Moved to Concord, Massachusetts.
　　　Married Lydia (Lidian) Jackson, September 14.

1836—Charles Emerson, brother, died May 9.
　　　Waldo Emerson, son, born October 30.
　　　Nature published.

1837—Gave Phi Beta Kappa address, "The American Scholar," at Harvard, August 31.

1838—Gave "The Divinity School Address" at Harvard, July 15.

1840—First issue of *The Dial* published in July.

1841—*Essays, First Series* published.

1842—Waldo Emerson died January 27.

1844—*Essays, Second Series* published.
　　　The Dial ceased publication in April.

1847—*Poems* published.

Sailed for England, October 5.

1848—Lectured in England and Scotland.

Went to Paris.

1850—*Representative Men* published.

Began his lecture tours in the West.

1855—The Saturday Club founded.

1857—*The Atlantic Monthly* founded in November.

1866—Given LL.D. by Harvard.

1867—*May-Day and Other Pieces* published.

Made an Overseer of Harvard.

Gave Phi Beta Kappa address, "The Progress of Culture," at Harvard, July 18.

1870—Gave course in philosophy at Harvard.

1871—Went to California.

1872—Concord home burned.

Sailed for Europe with daughter, Ellen, in October.

1875—Made Associate Member of the French Academy.

1882—Died April 27 in Concord.

Cabot, James Elliot. *A Memoir of Ralph Waldo Emerson,* 2 vols. Boston and New York: Houghton Mifflin Company, 1887.

Conway, Moncure Daniel. *Emerson at Home and Abroad.* Boston: James R. Osgood and Company, 1882.

Emerson, Edward Waldo. *Emerson in Concord.* Boston: Houghton Mifflin Company, 1888.

————, *The Early Years of The Saturday Club, 1855–1870.* Boston and New York: Houghton Mifflin Company, 1918.

————, and Forbes, Waldo Emerson, eds. *Journals of Ralph Waldo Emerson.* 10 vols. Boston and New York: Houghton Mifflin Company, 1909.

Emerson, Ralph Waldo. *Complete Works.* Centenary Edition, 12 vols. Boston and New York: Houghton Mifflin Company, 1903–4.

Garnett, Richard. *Life of Ralph Waldo Emerson.* London: Walter Scott, 1888.

Gregg, Edith W., ed. *One First Love: The Letters of Ellen Louisa Tucker to Ralph Waldo Emerson.* Cambridge, Mass.: The Belknap Press of Harvard University Press, 1962.

Holmes, Oliver Wendell. *Ralph Waldo Emerson.* Boston: Houghton Mifflin Company, 1885.

Harrison, John S. *The Teachers of Emerson.* New York: Sturgis and Walton Co., 1910.

Perry, Bliss, ed. *The Heart of Emerson's Journals.* Boston: Houghton Mifflin Company, 1926.

Rusk, Ralph L., ed. *The Letters of Ralph Waldo Emerson.* 6 vols. New York: Columbia University Press, 1939.

Sanborn, F. B. *The Personality of Emerson.* Boston: Charles E. Goodspeed, 1903.

Woodberry, George E. *Ralph Waldo Emerson*. New York:
The Macmillan Company, 1907.
Woodbury, Charles J. *Talks with Ralph Waldo Emerson*.
New York: The Baker Taylor Co., 1890.